GROW
IT!

RUTH BINNEY

GROW IT!

Everything You Need for a Successful Allotment

RP
RYDON
PUBLISHING

A Rydon Publishing Book

35 The Quadrant

Hassocks

West Sussex

BN6 8BP

www.rydonpublishing.co.uk

www.rydonpublishing.com

First published by Rydon Publishing in 2025

A CIP catalogue record for this book is available from the British Library.

ISBN: 978-1-910821-46-6

Printed in the Czech Republic by FINIDR, s.r.o

Contents

Foreword

There is nothing quite like an allotment. Even when you find yourself making jam or freezing beans at midnight, the satisfaction of growing and eating what you've grown super fresh, and being part of an allotment community, are unique to gardening.

In my life with plants, I have been lucky enough to cultivate, with my late husband Donald, two allotments in different parts of London – Dukes Meadows in Chiswick and in Highgate – and a third in Dorchester opposite Thomas Hardy's Max Gate. This book is a result of personal experiences and the expertise of dozens more allotment gardeners I have talked with over the years. My great thanks are due to them as well as to my publisher Robert Ertle and designer Prudence Rogers.

Gardening knowledge and practice, including no-dig cultivation and the introduction of new varieties continue to evolve, and I have included as many of these as possible to help bring success on any plot. The emphasis is on growing organically and with an eye to biodiversity. Here, too, are many ideas for enjoying your allotment harvest, with essential recipes for jam, chutney and other preserves.

With *Grow It!* to hand my wish is that you will have every success with your own allotment adventure. If you are still on the list – be patient. It will be worth the wait.

Ruth Binney, Cardiff, 2025

A Plot to Love

Day by day and year by year, and through successes and failures, an allotment is a unique and pleasurable way of gardening. It is undoubtedly hard work – but food for the soul and great exercise into the bargain.

TIME, ENERGY AND DEDICATION

An allotment is a commitment that will change the way you organize your life, but without time and dedication the weeds will quickly take over and you may become disheartened. Keep at it, and your energy will be rewarded with the joys of success, season by season. If you are lucky enough to have a gardening partner, it is much easier to share all that a plot demands.

A SPECIAL PLACE

An allotment is extra special if you have nowhere else to grow fresh fruit and vegetables, and you can even add some flowers into the bargain. This is a haven where you can watch things grow, and a place to have time to yourself or share it with your family of all ages. Cultivating your own plot, and eating your produce fresh, tasty and in profusion (or preserved for the winter) are the bonuses for being outdoors in the fresh air, appreciating nature, taking exercise and getting the soil under your fingernails. Not only are your crops the essentials of a healthy diet, packed with nutrients of all kinds, but you know exactly how they have been grown and can guarantee them free of unwanted chemicals.

At any allotment, the state of the weather and the rampaging of rabbits are far more vital than any gardener's wealth or social standing. Allotments are also rescue remedies – for the retired, the redundant, the lonely and the bereaved, where the important things in life are the weeds, slugs and snails. Here sharing

is the norm – of expertise, physical help and the exchange of plants and produce. The urge to cultivate the land is universal, and the competitive instinct to be the gardener with the best and biggest crops undeniable, but allotment gardening is subtly different in town and country. If you have no more than a window box, then the allotment is as important for relaxation as for digging and growing. Town and city dwellers undoubtedly keep drinks, mugs and plates in their sheds more often than country gardeners.

Allotment societies vary, but many organize communal events, including barbecues and parties as well as shows and competitions. If the plots are owned by the council or run by an active association, they may carry out annual inspections in late summer and award prizes for the best tended and most varied plots, or they may organize regular shows. These are the opportunity to display the best of your produce as well as to learn about the qualities of prize-winning examples, prepared and displayed to RHS standards.

CHILDREN AND PETS

While you are devoted to your allotment, don't assume that your children will want to spend hours there in foul weather helping you dig and plant, but if they do, consider yourself blessed. You may be able to make a sandpit to keep young ones entertained, and on a newly acquired plot, stone picking, and hunting for old bits of crockery, coins and other treasure can be fun. Encourage children to sow seeds of quick growing vegetables like radishes and lettuce in their own patch, but check whether they actually like the vegetables they're growing. On this score peas, though they take longer to mature, can be a much better choice than radishes.

When it's cold, a place for kids to sit in a shed is a bonus, and a hot summer's day, there are few who won't love watering and hosing. Harvest time is an ideal opportunity to get children engaged – though for strawberries, raspberries and peas, be prepared for plenty of eating, too. Another good entertainment is scratching initials on a young marrow or pumpkin and watching them expand.

Much as you love your dog, always keep the territories and sensibilities of your neighbours in mind. There may even be rules about bringing dogs to the plot and keeping them on leads. No dog will be welcome that wanders over other people's allotments or even fouls them, nor will one that barks a lot or terrorizes children. Always keep a water bowl in your shed for a dog. If you have a problem with a neighbour's dog, try the friendly approach. As a last resort you may need to report the problem to your committee.

Plot invasions by neighbouring cats are virtually impossible to control. As well as roaming the allotments, cats will use plots as lavatories and on a sunny day you may even find one asleep among your herbs. On the plus side, feline hunters will help catch rats and mice in and around allotment sheds.

"This is a haven where you can watch things grow, and a place to have time to yourself...."

WELCOME WILDLIFE

Even in a city, being at an allotment is almost like enjoying the country. The pristine allotment is going to be less wildlife friendly than one where at least a few areas are allowed to get seedy and overgrown – so weigh up your priorities with a keen eye to biodiversity. Creatures to deter can be found with pests and diseases (see p 51) and with the various plant groups.

Bees

Always welcome, bees are vital for pollinating flowers and producing crops of everything from courgettes and cucumbers to peas and beans, apples and pears. You may be lucky enough to have a beekeeper on your site, but if not, do your best to attract them. The flowers of blackberries, raspberries, loganberries and gooseberries are bee magnets, as are those of borage, thyme, marjoram, mint and sage and other pretty herbs.

top tip

If you grow rocket in succession, let one planting bolt and flower to attract bees. Although they are weeds, poppies, dead nettles and speedwells all have bee-friendly blooms. They will also attract useful wasps.

Wasps

The chief benefit of wasps is that the colony's workers devour large quantities of insects, which they feed to developing grubs in return for meals of the sugary saliva the grubs produce. They become a nuisance only towards the end of the season when the grubs have matured and flown the nest, and they have to seek out sweetness from plums and other fruit. Leaving some windfall apples on the ground for wasps to feed on will help to distract them from your picnics.

Hoverflies

Hoverflies look like wasps without 'waists' and hover motionless over plants. The grubs devour huge numbers of aphids while the adults are excellent pollinators.

Ants

Tireless scavengers, helpful for decomposing and recycling organic matter, however ants will kill and eat caterpillars. Many encourage aphids by 'farming' colonies for nectar and protecting them against ladybirds..

Ladybirds

Red, yellow or orange, spotted in black, ladybirds are good allotment scavengers. Both the adults and their larvae, dubbed 'garden crocodiles', can devour up to 150 aphids in a single day.

Frogs and toads

Damp patches in the allotment, and the moist shelter of large leaves, are most conducive to frogs and toads, as are ponds. These allotment friendly creatures will devour insects by the hundred but can be the subject of severe phobias.

Butterflies

As long they are not cabbage whites laying eggs on your brassicas, butterflies are most welcome for their beauty and as pollinators. To attract butterflies, plant a buddleia (which bees also love) and encourage a patch of nettles, a plant favoured by the caterpillars of peacocks, red admirals and small tortoiseshells. Grasses allowed to flower around plot perimeters will attract meadow browns and small heaths.

Hedgehogs

Although they feed on valuable worms, hedgehogs will also eat slugs, beetles and the like. Once resident at the allotment hedgehogs will not need extra feeding but will appreciate a pile of leaves or other vegetation in which to hibernate over winter.

Worms

Earthworms are invaluable. Except in the depths of winter they continually till the soil, helping to produce a fine tilth, loosening, rotating and aerating the soil and eating earth containing leaves and other organic material then excreting the remains. To encourage more worms, always keep your soil moist and regularly add plenty of organic matter. In a compost heap, the best worms to encourage are red brandlings (*Eisenia foetida*). Other helpful worms are nematodes, key weapons in organic pest control.

Spiders

In the autumn (their mating season) allotment dew-covered spiders' webs are everywhere to be seen, often attached to long strings of gossamer, spread plant-to-plant. Spiders are welcome all year for their ability to catch and eat insects. In spring, look out for the magical 'hatching' of new generations from egg sacs.

Birds

It is always a thrill when a robin lands beside you as you work, and as long as you keep them off your fruit and young plants, birds do much good by eating unwelcome invertebrates. Feeders will attract blue tits, finches and other small birds, but also unwelcome pigeons, so the choice is yours. Buzzards, now more numerous in many areas, may even visit and will catch mice and other rodents.

Foxes

Allotment foxes are pests only if they do damage by digging up young plants as they bury surplus food. Mangy individuals can be a distressing sight you may need to report to your local authority or RSPCA. It is unwise to feed them. On a rabbit infested plot foxes are welcome; they will also catch and eat rats, mice and squirrels. On the minus side, hedgehogs, frogs and birds appear on the fox's menu.

Rarer sightings

It is a thrill to find rarer wildlife on your plot, whether hummingbird hawk moths – visitors to southern Britain in warm summers – or adders, lizards or newts. Slow worms are also welcome consumers of slugs and snails but will appreciate long grass or a log pile to hide in.

WILDFLOWERS

Allowing some weeds to flourish in the allotment will encourage visits from butterflies and other insects and provide dark, damp areas for creatures such as frogs. You can also use a good crop of nettles to make your own organic fertilizer and young nettle and dandelion leaves are tasty salad ingredients. Even if you don't like weeds on your own plot, the allotment perimeter can be a diverse habitat for wild plants. You may even find plants like raspberries seeding themselves on your plot.

top tip

If you're uncertain about the weather, keep an eye on any scarlet pimpernels. If the flowers close up before two in the afternoon (their daily closing time) then it is almost sure to rain.

top tip

If you should see an adder, Britain's only poisonous snake, which may be sunbathing on your plot to warm up in springtime, always leave it to its own devices.

THE ALLOTMENT SHED

The good shed adds huge pleasure to the allotment and may even reflect allotment history as at Wolverton, near Milton Keynes, where the oldest sheds were made from parts of railway carriages. Ranging from luxury 'chalets' to ramshackle constructions, sheds reflect the character of a plot and the skills of recycling – sheds built entirely from wood foraged from skips and dumps are not unusual. Whatever type of shed you have, be sure that it is constructed or its base protected in such a way that rats or other wildlife are unable to make homes underneath.

For a new shed, there are many options from fully constructed to flatpack, but you will always need a good base and a structure secure enough to survive gales. If wooden, it should also be treated with a preservative to prevent rotting. A pitched roof covered with bitumen sheeting, or something similar, is essential to help keep it watertight. Guttering that allows for water collection is a desirable bonus. Windows of plastic or glass (if allowed) are an optional extra but need to fit very well to be watertight and avoid wind damage. A door that you can secure from the inside is helpful for privacy and shelter.

Tools of all kinds will be stored in the shed, along with everything you need for watering, protecting, supporting, feeding and labelling your plants at every stage of their growth. These range from fleece (and pegs to hold it down) to netting of different grades and buckets or big plastic bins for carrying weeds, compost and the like. Be sure to keep 'chemicals', even organic ones like chicken pellets, out of children's reach. Then add everything you need for picnics, tea making and relaxation.

Even if your plot is behind locked gates, add a heavy duty padlock for the shed. The theft of allotment tools is a recurring issue in both town and country. The police advise clearly etching or marking your allotment or home postcode on all your tools.

THINGS TO KEEP IN YOUR SHED

<u>ESSENTIAL</u>
· A first aid kit.
· Compostable wipes. Also handy if you cook and eat at the plot or often have children there.
· Tissues enclosed in secure plastic bags.

<u>USEFUL ADDITIONS</u>
· Scissors – for cutting everything from string and fleece to topping and tailing gooseberries and trimming spring onions.
· Sharp knife – for trimming vegetables and cutting off woody roots.
· Screwdriver – for odd jobs such as tightening a hose attachment.
· Animal proof containers for seed packets.

· Plastic bags – for taking produce home.
· Large plastic sacks – for non-compostable weeds and diseased plant matter that need to be disposed of away from the plot.
· Plastic food containers – ideal for fruit. Those with holes in the base are good for germinating seeds and raising seedlings.
· Plastic bottles – cut down to put as guards on tops of sticks and for watering.
· Kneeling pad – to save wear and tear on the joints.
· Folding chairs, plus picnic gear. Barbecue equipment if it is allowed.

Visitors

As well as friends and neighbours you'll almost certainly have to share your shed with other living creatures. Mice will take shelter and nest in your shed where they will eat any unprotected plant material, including the paper of seeds packets and their contents. Rats can also enter through holes and are much less welcome. They are endemic on most city allotments but particularly attracted to any site where edible scraps have been put on open compost heaps. A shed may be a shelter for overwintering butterflies which will flutter out on a sunny spring or winter day and spiders whose young will hatch in spring. Or birds may treat your shed like a giant nesting box.

top tip

BEWARE!
Be very careful about keeping inflammable liquids such as barbecue fuel in a shed. They are extremely hazardous.

Allotment Knowhow

There is a great deal
you need to know before
and after taking on an
allotment. If the waiting
list is long you may
be able to share with
someone to see exactly
what it entails.

The ideal allotment is the one closest to your home and most likely to be owned by the council, who you should contact in the first instance. They will almost certainly have rules about postcode eligibility. Some sites are privately owned, too, so always ask around, but best of all, contact The Allotment Society who will have all the relevant information for your area.

MAKING THE DECISION

When you are finally offered a plot, think carefully about whether you really have the time and energy to carry out all the work involved. Do the plots look well tended? Is it secluded, secure and likely to be free from thieves and vandals? Will council, landlord or allotment rules allow you to erect a greenhouse or dig a pond? When you are shown around the site ask as many questions as possible about the soil and growing conditions and take note of which crops are looking most healthy. Enquire about resident pests such as rabbits.

Most council and allotment associations conduct inspections once or twice a year to see whether plots are being properly looked after. If they're not, then they will issue 'dirty plot' warnings and give a deadline by which improvements must be made. This is the point at which you will have to decide whether to continue.

top tip

Think twice about taking on allotment full of perennial weeds such as horsetails that are virtually impossible to eradicate. Extremely exposed and hilly sites, and those with overhanging trees are also questionable choices.

MORE QUESTIONS TO ASK

• What is the rent and when and to whom is it payable?
• How often are plots inspected for their condition?
• Is a key needed for access, and if lost how can it be replaced?
• Is there a shop or trading post for members selling materials, and do they give discounts?
• Does the site hold shows and competitions, parties and barbecues?
• What are the rules about greenhouses, bonfires and the use of weedkillers and pesticides?
• Are working parties organized for big jobs on the site, if these are not done by the council?
• Are you allowed to sell any produce you grow on the plot?

BEGINNINGS

So you have your plot. Unless it is brand new and the ground has been prepared for you in advance it probably won't have been cultivated for some time, and even if it has been rotovated that certainly won't have eliminated the weeds. The first thing you will need to do is to clear it, at least in part. If you are going to cultivate 'no-dig' (see p 37) which can take several years to get going properly, you are unlikely to want to clear the entire space immediately, but even having space for a first crop of radishes or lettuces is a real bonus. It may be tempting to rotovate a plot, especially if it is full of perennial weeds, but beware. The rotovator will cut the roots up into tiny pieces and spread them around.

On large sites, allotments are usually allocated to newcomers in autumn or winter so that new tenants have the time to clear and dig the site before weeds burgeon again in the spring. Patience is almost certainly a key requisite. Even so, it may take months – or years – of dogged cultivation to get the plot into the shape you want.

Taking time to plan the plot, and where you want to put raised beds, fruit bushes and trees and other permanent plantings such as asparagus and Jerusalem artichokes will always pay dividends. You may also want to make space for a new shed, flower garden and, if allowed, a greenhouse. The ends of the plot are often good choices for permanent plantings but may be exposed to wind on an open site.

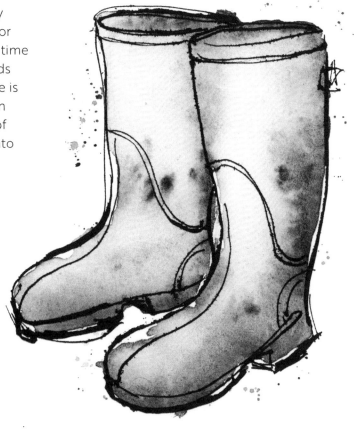

CROP ROTATION

Vitally, you need to build into your plan the need for crop rotation. The principle behind this is that moving plants around the plot helps to keep your soil in tip top condition and prevents the build up of specific pests and diseases such as club root in brassicas and eelworm in potatoes. Ideally, you will only grow the same thing in the same position every four years.

Perfect crop rotation can be tricky if some parts of your plot have better soil, or are less windy, and overwintering brassicas like purple sprouting broccoli will still be in the ground by the time you are sowing seeds of crops like peas, beetroot and parsnips in spring. Sweetcorn, salads, courgettes, squashes and cucumbers, as well as herbs like rocket and basil, can go in anywhere you have space.

Grouping your crops

Keep like with like in your rotation plan using these divisions:
• Brassicas: Brussels sprouts, broccoli, cabbage, cauliflower, kale, kohlrabi, swedes, turnips.
• Legumes: Peas plus broad, French and runner beans.
• Onion family: onions, garlic, shallots, leeks.
• Potato family: potatoes and tomatoes.
• Roots: beetroot, carrots, celeriac, celery, parsley, parsnips, radishes (not swedes and turnips).

A FOUR YEAR PLAN

Divide your plot roughly into four and use this planting scheme for rotation

YEAR 1	YEAR 2
Bed 1 Potato family	Bed 1 Onion family and roots
Bed 2 Onion family and roots	Bed 2 Legumes
Bed 3 Legumes	Bed 3 Brassicas
Bed 4 Brassicas	Bed 4 Potato family

YEAR 3	YEAR 4
Bed 1 Brassicas	Bed 1 Legumes
Bed 2 Potato family	Bed 2 Brassicas
Bed 3 Onion family and roots	Bed 3 Potato family
Bed 4 Legumes	Bed 4 Onion family and roots

WHAT WILL YOU GROW?

The answer is whatever you and your family like to eat – and what you're able to store, freeze or preserve over the winter. The time you have for gardening is also a consideration. As well as the familiar favourites you can also experiment with new and heritage varieties and more unusual crops to see how they do and whether you like them. The soil on your plot, the weather – and the protection you're able to provide for the more tender plants – will also have a bearing on what you grow.

MONTH BY MONTH
Use this basic guide to plan activities.

□ Control weeds, compost non-diseased plant matter but discard rooted perennial weeds
□ Water and mulch as necessary
□ Choose disease and bolt resistant cultivars

All Year

□ Harvest winter brassicas
□ Start forcing rhubarb
□ Sort out the shed, clean and sharpen tools
□ Plant bare rooted fruit bushes if weather allows
□ Lightly prune apple trees
□ Prune gooseberries
□ Plan crop rotation

January

□ Begin chitting seed potatoes
□ Plant and/or divide rhubarb
□ Mulch asparagus and Jerusalem artichokes
□ Cover some soil with cloches or polythene to warm
□ Prune autumn raspberries and blackcurrants
□ Cut back perennial herbs

February

March

- [ ] Hoe off annual weeds as they appear
- [ ] Sow tomatoes and cucumbers indoors
- [ ] Sow peas under fleece or cloches
- [ ] Sow leeks in modules
- [ ] Plant asparagus crowns
- [ ] Plant onion sets
- [ ] Plant comfrey for green manure
- [ ] Remove aphids on new growth (ideally by hand)
- [ ] Prune blueberries

April

- [ ] Sow beetroot, carrots, Swiss chard, cauliflowers (summer), kohlrabi, lettuce, radish, turnip, spring onions and peas
- [ ] Plant first and second early potatoes
- [ ] Sow and plant leeks
- [ ] Thin out vegetable seedlings
- [ ] Plant chitted potatoes
- [ ] Plant Jerusalem artichokes
- [ ] Sow marrows, courgettes, pumpkins and squashes indoors
- [ ] Start tomatoes and cucumbers indoors
- [ ] Sow and net brassicas
- [ ] Harvest rhubarb
- [ ] Set up supports for peas and climbing beans
- [ ] Sow parsley indoors
- [ ] Spread any well rotted compost from the bin

- [ ] Remove weeds as they appear
- [ ] Sow French and runner beans under cover or directly from mid month
- [ ] Sow parsnips
- [ ] Continue sowing carrots, beetroot, radish, lettuce etc
- [ ] Sow winter crops such as cabbage and broccoli in modules
- [ ] Thin out vegetable seedlings
- [ ] Plant late potatoes, earth up early varieties
- [ ] Harvest asparagus
- [ ] Protect strawberries before they ripen
- [ ] Net fruit bushes
- [ ] Harden off tender vegetables eg French beans, tomatoes, courgettes then plant out later in the month
- [ ] Plant out celery, cucumbers, tomatoes and cucurbits raised indoors
- [ ] Hoe regularly

- [ ] Keep on top of weeds
- [ ] Repeat sow carrots, beetroot, radish, lettuce, etc
- [ ] Make your own fertilizer from, eg, nettles or comfrey
- [ ] Transplant leeks
- [ ] Sow French and runner beans direct into the soil
- [ ] Sow or plant out sweetcorn, sow Florence fennel
- [ ] Repeat sow beetroot, spring onions, radishes, herbs and salads
- [ ] Plant out courgettes, pumpkins, marrows and squashes raised indoors
- [ ] Feed tomatoes and train, pinching out side shoots on cordon types
- [ ] Protect fruit crops with netting
- [ ] Harvest peas and first early potatoes
- [ ] Sow and plant basil and other tender herbs

July

- [ ] Sow pak choi and other oriental vegetables
- [ ] Sow spring cabbage in modules
- [ ] Remove side shoots from tomatoes regularly
- [ ] Lift and dry garlic, and onions if mature
- [ ] Lift first and second early potatoes
- [ ] Harvest globe artichokes
- [ ] Harvest early fruiting raspberries and prune out old canes that have fruited
- [ ] Pick courgettes regularly while small
- [ ] Trim gooseberries and currants lightly ahead of harvest
- [ ] Make 'home grown' fertilizer

August

- [ ] Sow salad crops, also spinach (mild areas) and kohlrabi
- [ ] Sow spring cabbages
- [ ] Trim perennial herbs
- [ ] Remove growing tips from tomatoes once 4 trusses have formed
- [ ] Lift and dry onions
- [ ] Harvest courgettes regularly
- [ ] Harvest beetroot, carrots, radishes and other salad crops
- [ ] Turn the compost heap and water if necessary
- [ ] Preserve crops for winter use

September

- [ ] Sow winter salads, eg lamb's lettuce, rocket in sheltered spot
- [ ] Sow green manure eg grazing rye (*Secale cereale*)
- [ ] Net brassicas
- [ ] Harvest remaining green tomatoes
- [ ] Transplant spring cabbage
- [ ] Peg out and plant strawberry runners
- [ ] Harvest apples, pears, sweetcorn, autumn raspberries
- [ ] Harvest and store pumpkins and squashes
- [ ] Pick and dry herbs

- [ ] Cut back beans and peas to ground level (leave roots in the ground)
- [ ] Pull up remains of spent vegetable crops and add to compost with other vegetable tops
- [ ] Sow winter hardy broad beans
- [ ] Plant peas in containers and place under cloches
- [ ] Harvest late pears
- [ ] Plant garlic, shallots and hardy overwintering onions
- [ ] Sow green manure
- [ ] Plant fruit trees
- [ ] Divide established rhubarb plants
- [ ] Harvest and store final maincrop potatoes
- [ ] Clear soil after harvest and sow green manure, or mulch with compost or weed suppressing fabric

- [ ] Plant raspberries, gooseberries, currants, also well rooted strawberries
- [ ] Plant out and net spring cabbages
- [ ] Harvest leafy crops before cold weather sets in, eg kale, chard, turnips, also cauliflowers
- [ ] Harvest swedes, parsnips (protect if necessary)
- [ ] Stake and harvest Brussels sprouts
- [ ] Prune apple and pear trees
- [ ] Clean gardening 'kit'
- [ ] Add fallen leaves to a leaf only compost heap

- [ ] Plant rhubarb
- [ ] Harvest Brussels sprouts, leeks, parsnips
- [ ] Keep brassicas well netted
- [ ] Order bare rooted fruit trees
- [ ] Browse catalogues for best and new varieties

TOOLS

Good tools will always be a wise investment, but be sure to try them by hand before you buy for weight and ease of use, depending on your height and strength. As well as the standard spades, rakes and forks (both standard and hand-held), hoes are essential for weeding. These come in various designs so you may want to experiment to see which suit you best. A Dutch hoe, with a flat, thin blade is the classic weeding hoe, while a draw hoe has a blade at right angles to the handle. There is also a short-handled version, traditionally called an onion hoe, which is good for working close to plants. Trowels can be wide or slim. One of each will always be handy; slim ones are often best for weeding and planting. A dibber is also useful for planting.

Secateurs and shears are other additions to the tool kit, plus a shovel for shifting compost. There are all kinds of specific weeding implements on the market that may suit you, and many adapted specifically for disabled gardeners. Cordless power tools such as rotovators and strimmers are useful (and often best borrowed), but check what is allowed at your site.

top tip

Always clean your tools as best you can at the allotment after you've used them, but take them home occasionally for a thorough wash and always in late autumn and early spring.

"Good tools will always be a wise investment...."

SOIL

To grow good produce you need a good layer of topsoil from which plant roots can absorb water and nutrients. If you're using no-dig cultivation, a good tilth will build up as the compost you put onto the soil rots down, and adding compost will always help to improve any shallow topsoil. The soil you acquire, though probably a mixture, will tend towards one of the four basic types – clay, chalk, sand or peat. Looking around your site will quickly show you what grows well, and it's worth asking the old hands about the allotment soil before you commit to your plot.

Even after many years of composting you may never achieve the ideal of porous, open nutrient rich loam that is the textbook ideal (technically a mixture of 20-25 per cent clay, 30-35 per cent chalk and 40-50 per cent sand), but it is worth persisting. Feeling the soil will give you an idea of its type and structure. Wet your hands, then pick up a handful of soil and roll it around. Clay will quickly form itself into a sausage shape while chalk or sand will break up.

Acid or alkaline?

From the start, and on a regular basis, it is worth measuring the acidity of your soil with a testing kit. For allotment fruit and vegetables the ideal soil, especially if you want to grow brassicas or root crops like turnips, is one that is slightly alkaline. A reading of anything above 7 is alkaline, below 7 is acid.

top tip

A very weedy allotment contains clues about the soil. Lots of creeping buttercups are a sign of waterlogged acid soil, while scarlet pimpernels and thistles flourish on chalk. Dandelions will grow almost anywhere but are most profuse on heavy soils. On the plus side, nettles are a sign that the soil is fertile and rich in nitrogen, as are fat hen, chickweed, couch grass and thistles.

Chalk

Chalky soil is virtually the opposite of clay and can look pure white when dry. It is flimsy and drains so quickly that even after a whole day's rain can be bone dry within 24 hours. Chalk's alkalinity can impair plant health, making growth poor and, when extreme, turning leaves yellow in a condition called chlorosis. Well rotted leaf mould, horse manure and garden compost all help to raise both the soil acidity and water retention. No lime is needed. Growing green manures is another good way of improving chalky soils and mulching helps too. Mulching moisture dependent plants with bark is also a great help on chalk soils.

Clay

Made up of fine particles, clay soil can be brown, grey or yellow. It retains water so well that it is slow to drain. When dry it forms a hard, thick cement like crust, making it almost impossible to work. It is also slow to heat up in spring, so poor for plants needing a good start. The great advantage of clay is that it is essentially very fertile, but because it is usually acid will almost always need lime added, particularly if you want to grow good brassicas, but allow at least month after liming before you put in plants or seeds. Mushroom compost, being alkaline, is great for clay soils. Any kind of grit will help break up clay and improve drainage, but best is pea shingle, horticultural gravel or coarse sand (but not the builder's variety). Digging in shredded newspaper can also help to break it up.

top tip

Grass cuttings make a quick mulch but never apply them more than 5 cm (2 in) deep or they will create too much potentially damaging heat.

top tip

Always keep liming well separated from manuring. The two react together to make unwanted, harmful ammonia.

Sand

The great advantages of sandy soil, which slips easily through the fingers, are that it drains well and warms up quickly in spring, making it ideal for early crops. Like chalky ones, sandy soils need plenty of organic material added to give them more bulk and to improve their water retention. Green manures and mulches are also ideal for sandy soils.

Peat

Dark and rich, peaty soils are naturally rich in humus but often have a poor structure which leads to inadequate drainage. Rather than adding loads of compost, coarse sand or pea shingle, as with clay soils, are best for improving peat. The soil is likely to be very acidic, needing the addition of lime, but will be ideal for growing blueberries.

COMPOST AND MANURE

Making good compost is a most satisfying job. But while it is easy enough to pile compostable green stuff in an allotment corner, it will quickly become unsightly and unmanageable. The first requisite for neat composting is a container. If you have space, create a double bin, with each section about a 1 m (3 ft) square, so that the contents of one can be rotting down while the other one is filling up. The classic design is of slatted wood – another use for old timber, skip finds and the like. Slotted slats on the front of each section make them easy to remove. Failing perfection, solid pieces of board will make satisfactory bin fronts.

A quicker way to make a serviceable composter is with reinforced chicken wire, though it needs to be solid enough to prevent the weight of compost collapsing the sides. If you only have space for a single bin, there are many plastic versions available including new, large, sealed 'self-powered' versions, that will keep the contents at 40-60ºC, so speeding up the decomposition process. The largest can deal with over 20 kg (44 lb) of organic waste in a week. Smaller bins are best emptied out completely every year or so. You can then remove what's useable and return the rest to the bin.

There are compost heap bonuses – both accidental and deliberate. You can plant potatoes direct into the heap, which can work well for an early crop of new potatoes, or use them for heat loving cucumbers, courgettes or cucamelons.

WHAT TO PUT ON THE COMPOST HEAP

• From the plot: Any healthy leafy material – dead leaves and soft vegetable trimmings, including rhubarb leaves.
Annual weeds.
Pods from shelled broad beans and peas.

• But not: Perennial weeds or very woody stems and roots – like old Brussels sprouts.
Diseased plants like blighted tomatoes – they should be destroyed or taken to the dump.

• From home: Vegetable peelings and eggshells; coffee grounds, tea bags and tea leaves; shredded woody material; shredded plain paper and thin cardboard; grass cuttings (within reason).

• But avoid: Fallen leaves unless you can compost them separately and give them two years to rot down. Also, meat and bones (magnets for vermin); animal litter and faeces; glossy, sparkly or embossed paper.

Compost step by step

If starting from scratch, put a layer of well rotted compost into the bottom of the bin to get it going. This will also contain helpful worms that eat, mix and digest organic matter. On top of this add alternate layers of wet waste (such as vegetable leaves and kitchen peelings) and drier material, ideally chopped up a bit. If you are adding grass cuttings layer them with dry material to prevent slime.

Covering a heap with polythene – weighed down with bricks or big stones to prevent it from being blown away – will help keep in the heat and stop it being flooded. A heap or bin that is too wet is slimy and reeks of ammonia and may also have clouds of insects hovering over it. Turning is the best remedy at any time, but autumn and spring each year are the most effective. If you have space and patience, you can keep a bin or heap exclusively for rotting down leaves into leaf mould. It will take at least two years to get good compost, but it is excellent stuff.

The wormery

If you are easily able to take your kitchen waste to the allotment a wormery is another good way to make compost. It will also accommodate a small quantity of grass cuttings. Rather than solid compost the wormery produces a concentrated liquid feed, which is drained off from the bottom of the composter as well as solid nutrient rich 'black gold'. The average wormery contains around 500 worms, which work their way up through a series of trays. You can buy in the worms you need but may well have them (they are small and red, and known as tiger worms or brandlings) already in some compost. The worms will be most active in spring and summer, and may not survive cold winters so it is worth covering the wormery with some kind of insulation in winter, putting it into the shed or even taking it home.

Buying it in

Most plot holders are unlikely to be able to make enough compost for even a small plot. Alternatives are most restricted in the city where, unless you live near a city farm, it may be impossible to get hold of rotted animal manure. The best solutions are mushroom compost, dried poultry manure (pellets) or concentrated manure sold under proprietary names such as 'Super Dug'. Mushroom compost is expensive and not great for chalky or alkaline soils while concentrated manure, while it goes

top tip

For additional activation, add a commercial product like Garotter or a homemade nettle manure. Make this by half filling a bucket with chopped nettles, topping it up with water and leaving it for 3 or 4 weeks to mature. Then water the drained solution (you will need a large colander) onto the heap.

a long way, does little to improve the water-retaining properties of light soil.

Country allotment gardeners have many more choices, and likely to have farmers, stables and smallholders willing to sell you well rotted animal manure (usually horse or chicken) by the bagful or trailer load or half load. However unless it is mixed with straw, horse manure will not rot down successfully, and needs to be at least two years old to be useable, so always check before you commit and ask around for good suppliers. If the entrance to your allotment is kept locked, someone will need to be available to receive a delivery.

top tip

Composted chicken manure pressed into compact pellets, which can be available in organic form, is best applied between February and the end of the growing season in October, to help enrich the soil and maintain its balance. The recommended 'dosage' is 50g (1¾ oz) per sq M (sq yard).

Grow your own – green manures

An allotment is an ideal place to grow green manure, a fast-growing leafy crop – often a legume whose root nodules have the advantage of fixing nitrogen into the soil – which is then dug straight into the ground. As well as improving soil fertility green manures, especially autumn sown ones, are good at mopping up the nutrients remaining after crops have been harvested and help to prevent them being washed away by rain. They also help to suppress weeds but on the minus side are highly attractive to slugs. Remember too that any brassica and legume varieties will need to be built into your crop rotation scheme.

Using manure

There are those who like to dig in manure in spring and others who favour spreading a layer of manure over the plot in the autumn and letting the worms and bacteria do their work over the winter so that it can be lightly forked in spring. This works well as long as your manure is really well rotted. If not, large lumps will make the ground unsuitable for root crops. Digging in manure during the autumn may help it rot but, particularly if your soil is fine and chalky, winter rain will leach out many nutrients.

Compost extra

Fine, really well rotted, compost can be sieved to make a good potting medium, either on its own or mixed with a proprietary peat free brand. Like manure, compost can be used on the surface or dug in and is a better top dressing for crops like asparagus. Light compost, either homemade or concentrated, is an ideal late winter treatment for overwintered crops like sprouting broccoli, cabbages and garlic. Later in the year, use it around leeks, courgettes and brassicas of all kinds.

GREEN MANURE PLANTING PLAN

You need at least a six week 'window' to make and use green manure. Look for mixtures of seeds and sow by hand before raking seeds into the soil. There is no need for neat rows. Except for clovers and phacelia, whose flowers attract helpful insect pollinators, green manures are best dug in before they flower. Then allow at least two weeks before sowing crop seeds.

• Summer: Buckwheat, and fenugreek if you have room between crops. These are good for smothering weeds but leave the soil very dry. Also try phacelia, bristle oats and bitter blue lupin.

• Late summer (before mid September): Radish, mustard alfalfa or clover, trefoil, grazing rye or winter field bean. Dig in by end of October, or leave them to get frosted over the winter.

• September: Ryegrass (grazing rye) and winter field beans. These will grow well all winter, then can be dug in during spring to release nutrients.

top tip

Manure mulches are especially good for shallow rooted fruit like raspberries and strawberries and for rhubarb, a notoriously greedy feeder. Mulch in late winter or early spring, well before they start into growth.

DIGGING – OR NOT

On a crisp, late autumn day there are few jobs more satisfying than digging the allotment. But there are increasingly conflicting views about the merits of digging, and how deep you should go. You also need to consider the soil, since very light soils can be damaged, and their water retention destroyed, by too much disturbance, and light soils should never be dug between April and September. It is always unwise to dig when it is very wet and soggy, and you should never touch the soil when it is cold and frozen.

Digging with a spade or fork turns and churns the soil and remains an effective means of helping to get rid of stones and perennial weeds, which you need to pick out meticulously as you dig, getting every little piece of root if you can. As you dig, add manure or compost. Once the ground has been cleared you can simply put a thick top dressing of manure onto it in autumn, leave the worms to do their work over the winter, then fork in the remainder in spring. This is especially good for light chalky or sandy soils.

For a large area, be systematic and have any compost or manure that you're going to add in a wheelbarrow nearby. If you are creating a trench, take the soil from this to the far end of the area you are working on to fill in the final one. Put compost or manure into this first trench, then cover it with the soil from the next trench, and so on.

HOW TO DIG

Everyone develops their own digging technique, but to spare strain on your back there are a few good tips.

· Keep the spade or fork at right angles to the soil, your back straight and your knees bent as you push into the ground.

· Don't try to move too much soil at once.

· When you need to remove weeds or stones, or add compost, be sure to bend your knees.

· Dig a small area at a time.

top tip

It is a good idea to throw perennial and annual weeds into separate buckets or big plastic 'baskets' as you work (if your ground is stony keep an extra one beside you for those). If you can isolate annual weeds, or have leafy remains to get rid of, put them straight into the bottom of a trench.

NO-DIG CULTIVATION

To grow plants successfully without disrupting the soil and the microorganisms, fungi, earthworms and other creatures is the principle behind no-dig gardening. To do it successfully you will need large quantities of organic matter, which can include well rotted leaf mould, green waste compost and bought in bags of peat free compost. It is best to start on a small area and see how it works for you, and allotment rules may not allow you to keep large areas covered.

For an uncultivated area

Cut down any weeds to ground level then cover the area with cardboard – not plastic or carpet. Then put on top a layer of compost at least 20 cm (8 in) thick and tread it down firmly. (Alternatively use horticultural membrane and put the compost mulch underneath it.) Make sure than no light can penetrate. Wait 6 to 12 months for the cardboard and compost to rot. Then hoe or fork it over very lightly before you plant.

For an already cultivated area

Spread a layer of compost at least 15 cm (6 in) thick onto the soil and firm it down. Then simply set plants into the composted area. For seed sowing, use a hand fork or rake to create an area of crumbly soil. Annual weeds should die off successfully in about 3 months, but you will need to remove marestail and other stubborn perennials, which should at least have weakened growth, by hand. Then every autumn add a further 5 cm (2 in) of compost after crops have been harvested and the ground cleared.

"Set plants started in pots into the composted area...."

FOOD FOR PLANTS

Good compost should provide most of the nutrients plants need but many will benefit from extra feeding, especially during peak growing times. Without enough food they not only fail to make new growth but have poor disease resistance. Some allotment vegetables, including tomatoes, leeks and onions, sprouts, cabbages and cauliflowers are notoriously greedy feeders so will need special attention. Plants may also need small amounts of vital trace elements essential to their health.

Extra feeds: choice and application

The amount of extra food your plants will need depends greatly on the type of soil you have and your method of cultivation. No-dig cultivation will greatly reduce plants' needs. However plants growing in fast draining chalk and sand are always likely to need much more food than those on clay or peat.

Feeds applied as powder or granules direct to the soil rather than being watered in are best forked in very lightly or left as a top dressing. If applied when the ground is wet they will get to plant roots most quickly. Never let granulated fertilizer come into direct contact with plants as it can scorch and damage them, and take care to sprinkle them as evenly as possible. Keep them well away from soil in which you are going to plant or have planted seeds and don't be tempted to add more than the recommended amount. Overfeeding, especially of vegetables such as beans, can stimulate them to make leaves in preference to fruits.

> ## top tip
>
> To make an all purpose liquid fertilizer, fill a cotton shoe bag with compost and soak it in a bucket of water for about a week, moving it around every few days to mix it well. If you need to squeeze it, wear disposable plastic gloves. The resulting rich, brown liquid can then be watered direct onto plants.

TYPES OF FEED

The extra feed you give your plants can be organic or inorganic but the better your soil the less feed you will need to give.

• Fish, blood and bone meal: Traditional organic fertilizers especially good when applied at the beginning of the growing season as they release their goodness slowly over the season. As a guide, allow about 120-180 g (4-6 oz) per sq m (sq yard).

• Seaweed: Organic and high in trace elements, but cannot be put direct onto the allotment and may not be legal to remove from the beach. It can be bought in a granular form, as an excellent top dressing, or as a concentrated liquid.

• Ready-prepared: Check the ingredients of these if you are gardening organically. Be sure to dilute and/or apply them strictly according to the manufacturer's instructions. Generally, these work fast, and should be used only just before and during the growing season. Special feeds are formulated for specific plants such as tomatoes, usually in liquid form.

• Foliar feeds: Watered onto plant leaves they will apply food quickly and directly. They come in both organic and non-organic (inorganic) forms; as always, follow the maker's instructions.

What feeds contain

With all feeds, the key symbols to take notice of are NPK – standing for nitrogen, phosphates and potassium. A good all-purpose fertilizer will contain them in the proportions of 18 nitrogen to 8 phosphate and 8 potassium and will also note the presence of magnesium and other trace elements such as boron. These are the chief qualities of each:

Nitrogen Especially vital to all plants with green leaves such as spinach and cabbage.
Phosphates Improve general health of plants. Also stimulate the growth of roots and the development of flowers vital to crops such as peas and beans.
Potassium Helps to improve resistance to pests and diseases as well as promoting the production of flowers and development of fruits.
Magnesium Essential for the production of the green pigment chlorophyll in leaves.
Manganese Often lacking in sandy and alkaline soils. Vital for the growth of healthy long lasting leaves and root formation in crops like beetroot and parsnips.
Iron Lack of iron hinders good leaf formation. It is most usually a problem on alkaline, limey soils.
Molybdenum Also key to good leaf formation, particularly in brassicas.
Boron Essential for root vegetables which without it turn brown and crack. Also needed by brassicas such as cauliflowers. If necessary, add borax, mixed with sand or soil, at 30 g (1 oz) per 20 sq m (20 sq yards).
Zinc Boosts plant vigour.
Copper Helps to firm up leaf surfaces, making them more resistant to pests and diseases.

SOWING AND PLANTING

Although not the purists' choice, it is perfectly acceptable to buy, or gratefully accept from friends, ready grown plants for your plot. While a huge proportion of produce can be grown from seed, it helps to have the space to raise seedlings of many plants indoors or in a protected environment at the allotment before planting them out.

Choosing seed

When buying seed, look to see whether varieties are labelled 'F1'. If F1 they will be more expensive, and there will be fewer seeds per packet because they will be the result of first generation crosses bred to emphasize a particular, often extremely useful characteristic such as disease resistance or early cropping. 'Ordinary' seed is better value and often just as easy to grow, but it is often worth paying more for better growing qualities. If you like to keep seed from one year to the next – runner and French beans, for example – remember that seeds from F1 varieties are not guaranteed to come true. You may also want to look for organic seeds, for old 'heritage' seeds and for foreign varieties such as French and Italian. Every year new and exotic vegetables come onto the market such as cucamelons, back radishes and pink kale.

Pots, trays and cells

Many vegetables do best raised from seed at home then planted out into the allotment once well established. When using containers, sow small seeds thinly, and bigger ones either singly or in pairs. Check planting depths with

> ## top tip
>
> Deep plastic containers from the supermarket are good for raising seeds. The best ones already have holes stamped in the bottom. To prevent seeds and seedlings getting over wet, and dying from damping off or rotting, a mixture of potting compost and vermiculite (70:30 approximately) makes a great growing medium because it maximizes drainage. You can use an all-purpose compost or a special seed compost.

seed packets and advice for specific vegetables. To get vibrant root systems going you need containers that are sufficiently deep. Pots are fine (with crocks added for good drainage), but for bigger seeds, cells are ideal. These hinged containers, which pack into a plastic frame, come apart easily for removing established plants. Covering them with cling film until the first signs of germination appear can help to speed up the process.

Before being put out into the plot, seedlings may need to be thinned in their containers by removing the weakest. They may also need potting on – transferring to larger containers. An old kitchen fork or pointed 'mini trowel' is handy for getting them out when you do this. Be sure to check both roots and shoots when selecting the healthiest seedlings. If you've begun the seeds in a specialist compost such as John Innes No. 1 you will need to upgrade at this point.

Hardening off

When seedlings of tender plants are raised indoors they need hardening off before they can be planted out. If you have a cold frame, keep it open during the day and close it at night. If you don't you will have to carry pots and trays outdoors in the morning and bring them indoors again in the evening. Watch out for slugs and snails, which can quickly converge on tender crops, especially in the last stage of hardening off when seedlings are left outdoors all night.

Straight into the plot

Even if you are planning to transplant seedlings they can be started in one or more areas set aside as a seedbeds. To get the fine soil it is best sieved then mixed with some fine peat free potting compost before you sow. Scatter the seeds over a small area and cover them with soil or use successive parts of a row to raise seeds. A warming covering of fleece, cloche or equivalent will help to get them off to a good start. Check whether vegetables respond to being moved. Some, such as parsnips, are always best sown direct into the place where they will mature and thinned out.

As a rule, the larger the seed to more deeply it needs to be planted. For small seeds like leeks and rocket a good

"Many vegetables do best raised from seed at home then planted out into the allotment once well established...."

method is to make a shallow furrow with the end of a trowel or dibber, sprinkle in the seeds and cover them lightly with soil. Seed packets usually give a recommended planting depth. Even if you are sowing in a block, it helps to use a line of string tied to sticks to ensure straight rows. Planting by eye is fine for sowings such a small patches of radishes, or for lettuce seeds that will later be transplanted. For larger seeds like peas and beans, you can either make a deeper trench for planting or place seeds into individual holes made with a pointed trowel or dibber.

After you've finished your sowing, always label what you've planted. Seeds will need gently watering in and protecting from slugs and snails – and other pests like birds and rabbits – which can munch off the tops as soon as they appear. To help seeds to get started quickly you may also want to cover them with cloches, polythene or fleece. To prevent accidentally treading on an area, make string 'fences' to guard seeded areas. If seeds don't come up, start again. Even planted late they will catch up.

Planting out

At the allotment, the guidelines for straight rows, labels and protection are much as for seed planting. Otherwise, make sure the soil is well dampened before you begin. For leafy, thirsty plants like brassicas and lettuces, pouring water into individual planting holes before inserting plants is essential, this is known as 'puddling'. You may also want to add a handful of concentrated manure and a sprinkling of mycorrhizal powder in each hole. It is sold as 'Root Grow'.

Rows or blocks?

The allotment tradition is for planting in rows, but even without raised beds planting in half rows or small blocks is a good idea. Growing plants like lettuces in a block can help reduce weeds and improve water retention. For some crops, such a sweet corn, a block is also essential to ensure fertilization.

Whatever your choice, make sure that large plants like brassicas have enough room to grow to maturity without competing with their neighbours for light and root room. Good spacing will also allow air to circulate and prevent the over humid conditions in which diseases like downy mildew thrive. A useful space saving tip is to stagger plants to maximize the space between them. You also need to make sure that you have enough space to weed properly between plants without trampling on your crops and to harvest them easily.

Bed construction

Raised beds need to be 1.2 to 2 m (4-6 ft) wide, depending on how long your arms are, making use of the space you have as well as possible. For the sides you can use timber planks or boards of any kind, but gravel boards (long treated planks) are very easy uses, as are interlocking plastic sections. Or use bricks, stones or any materials suitable for recycling. Two or three board depths will give you the height you need. If perennial weeds are a problem on your plot, line the beds with thick weed proof fabric or plastic. A base lining of pea gravel will also help drainage. You can then fill the bed with compost and/or topsoil. Whatever you choose it needs to be as weed free as possible.

RAISED BEDS

Many allotment gardeners swear by raised beds. They can help to combat the problem of perennial weeds and, if made to the right proportions, mean that you never have to tread on the soil to work the ground. And they don't need to be dug. What's more you can cover a raised bed with polythene or fleece to make a 'mega cloche' and provide the special conditions needed by plants like blueberries that will only grow on acid soil. Carrots are a perfect crop for raised beds as carrot flies rarely fly higher than 50 cm (20 in) from the ground.

WATER AND WATERING

Rain, except in excess, is always the best way of keeping plants well watered. It is unwise to choose an allotment without water on tap unless you live almost next door to your allotment, and can run a hose to your plot or have a reasonable way of transporting it. Consider whether you will be able to collect rainwater in an open tank or, preferably, from guttering on the shed roof into a water butt.

Water is usually supplied to allotments either via taps (ideally placed strategically over tanks) or self-fill tanks from which you scoop water with a can. The number of plots per tap or tank will vary from site to site, but one for four plots is about average. If you are allowed to hose, consider the needs of your neighbours. It is not unusual for 'water wars' to break out in very hot and dry spells. Watering cans – ideally two per person – are essential. A wheelbarrow can also be useful to carry them from a tank. If you are allowed a hose, use a reel to help

stop it kinking. The newest expandable hoses are excellent.

Watering well begins as soon as germination begins. For seedlings, you need a fine spray so that you don't dislodge their roots. When transplanting, pour water into each individual planting hole to give the roots maximum moisture

WATERING WELL

Good watering timing and technique can help make best use of your energy and the precious liquid.

• When it's hot, water in the evening or early morning to reduce evaporation from the soil and water loss (transpiration) from plants.

• Water well. It can be as damaging and stressful to plants to give them just a sprinkling of water than none at all.

• Don't over water. Give plants a chance to put down deep roots and establish themselves well. Overwatering can also encourage wilt and other fungal diseases.

• Give extra attention to shallow rooted and leafy plants and those like cucumbers whose fruit have a high water content.

• Water right to the roots rather than spraying water on to the leaves.

and minimize any slowing down of their growth. After transplanting, young plants are best watered little and often until established, which could be twice a day in hot weather. Young plants like fruit bushes and trees will benefit from watering spikes. These are sunk in near plants and allow water to get directly to the roots as you fill them.

top tip

Garden wisely to conserve water. Use mulches generously while the soil is damp to conserve the moisture in the soil below, plant thirsty short-lived plants like lettuces close together and use fleece over plants, especially in windy weather, to cut down water loss.

WEEDS AND WEEDING

Even when you've cleared your plot, dealing with weeds is a necessary chore essential to plant health. As they grow, weeds take goodness from the soil and if close to crops can entwine stems and roots, so further restricting growth. Unlike enclosed gardens, allotments are extremely vulnerable to weed seeds blowing in on the wind, especially if there are uncultivated plots nearby. The grass and other vigorous perennials in paths can also add to the problem. As you clear your plot you'll recognize the weeds that are likely to be most troublesome. Use an organic weedkiller only as a very last resort and remember that you will need to leave a week from any treatment before plants can be eaten.

"Watering cans – ideally two per person – are essential...."

KNOW YOUR WEEDS AND THE WAY THEY REPRODUCE

Dandelion Seeds and pieces of the long tap root.
Dock Seeds and pieces of root.
Convolvulus Creeping, deep set rhizomes.
Creeping buttercup Seeds and runners.
Creeping thistles Seeds and rhizomes.
Ground elder Shallow, rampant rhizomes.
Nettle Seeds and rhizomes.
Horsetail Deep set rhizomes and spores.
Couch grass Rhizomes and seeds.

Types of weeds

Weeds can be annual or perennial. The annuals are relatively easy to control, especially if you can hoe and weed regularly. Common allotment annual weeds include hairy bitter cress, chickweed, groundsel, sow thistles, speedwell, scarlet pimpernels and many others. They are characterized by producing many small seeds, which germinate rapidly, especially when the soil surface is dampened by rain.

Perennial weeds are much more of a problem because they spread both by seeds and by other means, including underground runners (modified stems) or rhizomes (modified roots), which can often penetrate as much as 1 m (3 ft) below ground. Many of these weeds will regenerate from tiny pieces of root and rhizome, making them virtually impossible to eradicate. Constant weeding should weaken them a little, but persistence is the best remedy.

Weeding

Everyone develops their own weeding technique, but whatever works for you be sure that you do not risk treading on your crops as you go. If the soil looks dry, it is wise to water before you weed (take off the top surface of the soil with a trowel first to see if it's damp beneath). A long handled hoe is good for getting at small weeds between rows, but you may need to go over the area afterwards and pick off by hand any that look as if they may re-root. To get close to plants without damaging them you need a short handled hoe, a trowel or a fork (either a hand fork or a regular one) as well as nimble fingers.

To save wear and tear on your back, get down on your knees for close weeding and use a kneeling mat if that helps. Keep containers nearby to collect and separate annual and perennial weeds and after you have finished, especially when weeding between small plants, water them well.

Suppressing weeds

Keeping weeds in the dark will help to prevent them growing and spreading. To do this you can cover weedy areas with thick, black polythene, though this is not guaranteed to get rid of persistent offenders like couch grass and horsetails, even after a year, and is discouraged or even banned on many allotments if the polythene covers more than a small area. Old carpet is also useful, but again check the regulations.

Mulching will also help to deprive weeds of light. A mulch can be organic, in the form of bark or compost, or you can use proprietary black matting (again check if it is allowed), which is ideal for areas such as a strawberry beds. The best way of using it is to weed thoroughly, lay it, then cut holes in it through which plants are inserted.

A traditional way of getting rid of annual weeds and even suppressing perennials is to plant potatoes or a quick maturing crop of green manure. Growing flowers may also help, because chemicals exuded by the roots of one plant restrict the growth of a neighbour. That is why you can plant nasturtiums to help kill couch grass and marigolds to get rid of ground elder and bindweed.

BOUNDARIES AND PATHS

When you take on your plot it should be obvious where it begins and ends. Very likely at least one edge of your plot will be grass. A solid path, if there is one, may be gravel or tarmac and in any kind of repair. You will need to consider how best to keep grass under control, possibly with proprietary edging of some sort. If you are lucky, your council or neighbours may mow the grass between plots, but even this is unlikely to get right up to the edges. With a hard path you may be able to scrape weeds off with a spade or, if the problem is extreme, isolate them enough to kill them off with an organic weedkiller. Some, like wild blackberries – or cultivated ones that have been propagated with the help of birds – may even be useful and trainable.

Paths within the allotment are essential to get around without damaging growing crops. Erecting raised beds will, of itself, define path routes, but it helps to demarcate at least four areas to allow for crop rotation and to have a bed specifically for seeds and herbs. Planks and stone slabs are ideal for keeping paths in order and bark is also useful.

TREES AND OVERHANGS

Good fruit trees on an allotment are almost always welcome, but otherwise are likely to create too much shade, sap valuable water from the soil and deposit tons of leaves on your allotment every autumn. Trees can also be home to unwelcome allotment wildlife like squirrels and pigeons. If you wish to remove a tree, or have its growth severely cut back, check first with your allotment

top tip

When planning the removal of a tree, find out about having the roots extracted. If left in place they will still provide an inhospitable barrier to most vegetables.

committee and/or the local council. It will always need to be a professional job.

Beneath existing trees, shallow rooted raspberries can be persuaded to thrive if they are given a generous top dressing of manure, or you may like to plant daffodils and other spring bulbs. So long as you can keep it confined, mint will do well under a tree. In autumn. leaves of deciduous trees that fall on your plot are best scooped up and composted in a separate bin, if you have the space, or bagged up for recycling. Pine needles are only fit for the dump as they are virtually impossible to rot down.

Trees growing outside the allotment boundary are the responsibility of the people on whose land they are growing, usually home owners or the local council. Although you are entitled to cut back any parts of them that overhang your 'property' this is a problem best dealt with by your allotment committee.

PLANT PROTECTION

Allotment plants need protection to prevent attacks from pests and to speed germination and plant growth. With the added warmth that cloches, cold frames and fleece provide you can have crops early in the season, even without a polytunnel or greenhouse. Although they will not give you full frost protection, these coverings also allow you to overwinter plants grown from seed in the autumn or harden off tender plants raised at home. Early in the year, cloches and fleece can be used to help heat the soil before planting. Sheets of polythene over wire frames – essentially mini polytunnels – can do the same job. Any glass or polythene you use needs to be kept clean to let in as much light as possible.

Cold frames

The cold frame is essentially a mini unheated greenhouse with a roof that opens to allow for watering and temperature regulation. You can buy frames ready made from hardwood glazed version to metal frames covered in polythene. They are not hard to make yourself from metal frames covered with polythene.

Cloches

Traditionally made from glass, most cloches sold now are of clear plastic. The oldest sorts are bell shaped covers for one large or a few small plants. You need to be able to lift and move them easily for watering and weeding, but they also need to be held in place firmly enough that they're not blown away at the first spring gale. When not in use, they are best stored in a shed. The best cloches come with 'feet' to keep them secure and vented ends that can be opened or closed. In a larger form they are sold as growing tunnels. The very smallest polytunnels, which are cloche size (they are sold by some suppliers as 'sectional tunnel cloches') have hinged frames that allow them to fold flat when not in use.

Fleece

Semi opaque horticultural fleece has the advantage of letting in both air and rain, but keeping out pests like flea beetle and carrot fly, and can be a boon if you are not able to water every day. In dry weather fleece also helps to slow evaporation. It comes in different thicknesses but always needs to be pegged down well as it is easily blown off by the wind. You can buy fleece by the metre or opt for ready made fleece tunnels complete with metal frames and draw string ends.

Netting

Fine mesh netting – 5 mm or less – is excellent for keeping off pests and, on exposed allotment sites, provides shade from the extremes of the sun, which is helpful for young crops, and helps to prevent the soil from drying out too quickly. Only the very finest mesh, however, will act as an effective barrier against carrot fly; it is sold under trade names such as 'Enviromesh'. It can be pinned to a wooden frame or used over the hoops used to support fleece or polythene.

Wider mesh netting will protect crops from birds, but for brassicas a smaller mesh is advisable for deterring cabbage white butterflies. While effective draped over plants and tied to canes, it is always best attached to a proper frame. You can make one yourself from treated timber or build one from a kit of metal rods with ball shaped 'joints'. There is virtually every option of size and quality available, depending on what you can afford.

PESTS AND DISEASES

Allotment pests and diseases come in many guises – large, small and virtually invisible. You will never be able to deter or exterminate them all, but you can attempt to minimize the damage they cause. Some pests are specific to or most commonly afflict particular vegetables and fruit, so are dealt with in that context, while others do their damage on a much wider scale.

Rabbits

Allotment rabbits will eat anything except strong-smelling vegetables like onions and leeks and can devastate an allotment overnight. They even make tunnels to get at root crops. While it is possible to protect individual rows or blocks of crops with netting, fencing is the only effective way of keeping rabbits off your plot, which it may pay to have installed professionally. In any event, do not underestimate rabbits' capabilities – they can jump.

The ideal rabbit-proof fence needs to be about 1 m (3 ft) high, made of wire mesh supported with stout posts. It also needs to be sunk well down, allowing about 30 cm (1 ft) of fencing below ground level. If you have a shed, make sure the netting goes right around its base – rabbits will happily shelter, or even 'nest' underneath one. It helps to add at least one gate, or devise some sort of hinging mechanism to make it easy to get in and out.

Deer

Deer are a problem in some country allotments, but impossible to shield from individual plots except with very high fencing, and an issue for the owners or managers of your site. Deer also carry ticks, the vectors of lyme disease, which make them a serious problem.

Squirrels

These are most likely to be a pest if mature trees grow around or on your site. Protein-rich vegetables such as broad beans, peas and sweetcorn are their favourite foods, and you may need to protect these with netting barriers about 1 m (3 ft) tall, covered over the top. Growing plants in blocks, not rows, makes this much easier to manage.

Moles

The last place you want to find molehills is in the middle of your plot, but if they live round about you may well be vulnerable. Unless you use traps, they are almost impossible to get rid of, and the more worms you have in your (healthy) plot the more they will like visiting. Consult your local council if moles are a severe problem.

Rats and mice

Rats and mice can invade your sheds, and will use anything from newspaper to strawberry straw for bedding and eat any seeds or crops left in there although they rarely eat onions. On the plot, mice will dig up and eat bean and pea seeds, especially if these are planted early in the year when there is little other food around. The old fashioned way of deterring them is to lay branches of gorse or holly over the ground after planting, but fleece or netting well pegged down is a better choice. These rodents are also partial to root vegetables such as beetroot.

top tip

For protecting newly planted seeds, keep birds off by weaving string across the bed, supported by a series of sticks. Bird scarers of all kinds, from scarecrows to old CDs hung from bean sticks, plastic strips and windmills, to plastic bottles put over the tops of stakes, are common on allotments. Try them but be prepared for birds to outwit you.

top tip

Keep a close eye on any space beneath your shed that could be a home for rat and mice families.

Birds

These beautiful creatures are unwelcome only when they eat your fruit and vegetables. Brassicas, especially when newly planted, are a magnet for pigeons, and blackbirds are chief lovers of soft fruit, particularly when the weather is dry and they need fluids. Netting is the best deterrent.

Slugs and snails

Of all garden pests, slugs have the worst reputation as they will attack plants both above and below ground. The wetter the weather (or the more assiduous your watering) and the younger, softer and juicer a leaf or fruit, the more likely it is to be attacked. There are about 40 species of slugs in the UK but only a few actually damage plants. The remainder are extremely useful for breaking up organic material. Leopard slugs are even cannibalistic. The worst offenders are garden slugs with orange undersides to their bodies and grey field slugs that are either grey or light brown. Snails – notably over the winter – will congregate in the dark shelter provided behind anything from a plank of wood to the undersides of plant pots.

Other pests

For pests specific to particular plants:
Aphids, caterpillars, cabbage root fly and flea beetle – see Brassicas (p 66).
Wireworms – see Potatoes (p 97).
Carrot fly – see Carrots (p 89).

TO CATCH A PEST

While a biodiverse plot will help to keep slugs down they do need to be prevented from destroying young plants, and advice to hunt them by torchlight is never going to be a practical possibility on an allotment. These may be worth trying:

· Put plastic bottles over individual plants: Effective, but only practicable for a very small crop and need to be removed for watering.

· Upturned grapefruit halves with holes cut in them: Good but can look unsightly. Need to be strategically placed.

· Beer traps: Quickly attract the pests, but a bother to maintain.

· Gravel and glass chippings, and similar commercial products: Needed in large quantities, and right up to plant stems. Often not practical on an allotment and won't deter slugs below ground.

· Copper rings: Good for any plants like tomatoes grown in pots.

· Spread coffee grounds around plants: Probably more effective as a high nitrogen fertilizer but worth a try.

· Make a pond: Frogs, toads and other residents will feed on slugs.

DISEASES

Nearly all the diseases that affect allotment plants are caused by fungi or viruses, but plants are also prey to bacterial infections. Often, diseases are spread by insects and other pests, and can be extremely persistent, lying dormant in the soil over the winter, ready to strike again in spring when new shoots are beginning to establish themselves. Wet, warm summers also create the prime conditions for diseases to thrive. Diseases specific to particular plant groups are described in context, but the most universal ones are included here.

top tip

Crop rotation will help to keep diseases at bay, but good hygiene is also key. Always remove any infected plant material as soon as you spot it and destroy it. Never put it on the compost heap. Tell someone what it is before you dump it. If garden waste collected at your recycling centre is made into compost they may prefer your infected rubbish to go to landfill.

FUNGAL INFECTIONS

The problems caused by many fungal infections are worst when the weather is cold and damp, which is why you need to be careful not to over water plants, particularly when young. Because they reproduce by means of tiny spores, which are blown in on the air from neighbouring plots and can lie dormant in the soil for many years, fungal infections can be very difficult to eradicate.

Downy mildew
Symptoms Fuzzy whitish patches on leaf undersides, especially in wet summers and autumns. Leaf surfaces, and the curds of cauliflowers, may be yellow and discoloured. Affected plants may die.
Treatment Set plants well apart to maximize air flow between them. Remove and destroy any affected leaves immediately. Help avoid soil contamination with crop rotation. There are no approved treatments.

Powdery mildew
Symptoms Most likely to affect fruit. Leaves become covered with a white, powdery mould, and are distorted. Fruit fails to set or, if it does, becomes cracked and split, often with brown patches.
Treatment Destroy affected plant material safely.

Stem rot
Symptoms Mostly affects marrows, squashes and cucumbers, but also tomatoes. Slimy brown patches appear on plant leaves before the fungus invades the stems.
Treatment Remove affected leaves as soon as possible. Destroy badly affected plants.

Root rot
Symptoms First signs are brown or yellow shrivelling stems. All types of beans and peas, cucurbits and tomatoes are likely victims.
Treatment Pull up and destroy affected plants safely. Ideally remove the infected soil or, at the very least, leave it uncultivated for two years.

Brown rot
Symptoms Turns crops brown after creating a cottony white mould on stems, leaves and fruit. Affects apples, and many vegetables, including courgettes, marrows and broad, French and runner beans.
Treatment On fruit trees, use an approved fungicide early in the season to prevent the infection taking hold. Prevent the infection lingering from year to year by destroying any diseased tissue.

Damping off
Symptoms A fungus that affects vegetable seedlings, making them keel over and die.
Treatment Water sparingly and always use sterilized pots and soil for seed sowing. Always test the soil to make sure it is quite dry before watering. For seedlings raised in pots, try watering them from below.

Other diseases
For diseases specific to particular plants:
Brassicas – see p 67.
Onion family – see p 101.
Potatoes – see p 96.
Tomatoes – see p 110.

Growing Vegetables

From everyday crops like potatoes, runner beans and carrots, to more exotic vegetables such as fennel, pak choi and sweet potatoes, almost any vegetables can be grown at the allotment. The better tended and prepared your soil, and the more meticulous you are about keeping weeds under control, the better your vegetables will be.

BEANS AND PEAS

Bean sticks in rows and wigwams are the epitome of the allotment landscape, and there are few vegetables to beat the allotment bean – whether runner or French, dwarf or climbing. Peas, too, are excellent on the plot. The trickiest part of cultivating these vegetables is getting good germination and protecting young plants from slugs, snails, mice, rabbits and other pests. Otherwise they are productive, reliable and delicious.

BROAD BEANS

Broad beans are one of the most rewarding allotment crops. For early beans, seeds can be sown in October or November and overwintered, though you need a variety specifically bred for the purpose such as 'Aquadulce Claudia'. February (if it is warm enough), March and April are sowing months for 'main' crops.

Growing routine

Overwintering is by no means foolproof but likely to be more successful if plants are started off in deep 12 cm (5 in) cells or troughs. If the season is cold you may get patchy results and plants straggly from being decimated by the wind, but it is a good way of saving space for the many spring and summer crops to follow, and for warding off disease. A fleece covering will help to keep them warm, or a polytunnel.

Well manured ground is best for broad beans, with seeds planted at 15 cm (6 in) apart and about 5 cm (2 in) deep in double rows about 23 cm (9 in) wide. Even if the soil is warm and dry enough to plant seeds directly, they will benefit from the protection of fleece until

Allotment Choice

Some of the best choices old and new include:

'Aquadulce Claudia' Ideal for autumn sowing. Long pods.

'The Sutton' Dwarf, good for windy sites. A heritage variety grown for over 100 years.

'De Monica' Early maturing, good yield.

'Giant Exhibition Longpod' Tall with up to 10 beans per pod.

'Jubilee Hysor' Ever reliable cropper.

'Luz de Otono' Can be sown in July for a late crop or overwintered.

'Crimson Flowered' Unusual deep red flowers. An ancient variety dating to 1777. Shorter pods.

'Karmazyn' Pink beans in an improved heritage variety.

they germinate, which if well pegged down will also help keep mice and voles away. In colder places, or when spring weather is very cold and damp, they can be germinated in pots, cells or a deep seed tray. Sowing in succession every few weeks will extend the cropping season significantly.

Broad beans don't need much attention, but if your plot is exposed to wind they will benefit from good supports. A neat way of doing this is to push in sticks at about four-plant intervals, attach string to the end stick, then weave the string between the plants. As the beans increase in height you can add more string rows. Late plantings of broad beans are especially susceptible – and even more so in wet summers – to chocolate spot, a fungal disease whose name perfectly describes its symptoms. Once this strikes then the likelihood of getting a crop is virtually nil, so they are best pulled up and taken to the recycling centre.

top tip

Blackfly are usually the only serious pests of broad beans. Pinching the tops out of the plants will help, and will also give you bigger pods. Do this as soon as you see signs of infestation or even earlier, when the leaves can be added to a salad or stir fry. In milder areas overwintering will mean that they're ready before the blackfly season begins. Allotment squirrels, particularly partial to protein rich foods, can rapidly decimate a broad bean crop, making netting essential, which needs to be supported on sticks about 1 м (3 ft) tall. Growing plants in blocks, not rows, can make this much easier.

"Well manured ground is best for broad beans...."

FRENCH BEANS

There are two ways of growing French beans – either as dwarf crops or as climbers. There are dozens of sorts to choose from, including flat and rounded pods, beans coloured in purple or yellow, and those like the haricot and borlotti bean intended to be left to mature and harvested for drying. 'Tepee' types have pods held on tall stems well above their foliage, making them easy to pick.

Being shallow rooted, French beans appreciate a well sheltered position, which is not always easy to supply on an exposed site. They are also vulnerable to frost, meaning that you need to plan your sowing and provide protection if necessary. Allow 8 to 12 weeks from sowing to harvest. To help provide the moisture they like it helps to earth up the soil around dwarf bean plants a little as they are becoming established. Slugs and snails will go straight for your young bean plants if they are not protected, as will rabbits. For climbing beans, use tall sticks as for runner beans.

top tip

French beans will germinate if planted directly into the ground, but irregularities of the weather, especially early in the season, lead to many 'blind' germinations with no leaves. It is much more reliable to sow them individually 2 cm (5 in) deep in pots or cells and to germinate them indoors, under cloches or in a frame, then plant them out in double rows 5 cm (2 in) apart, (or in a block) into soil well mulched with rotted organic matter. For a really early crop, you can begin sowing in April, then carry on making sowings well into the summer.

Allotment Choice

Some of the best French beans to choose from a very wide selection:

'Boston' High yield of round, dark green pods.

'The Prince' Many long, straight, flat pods.

'Dior' Copious yellow pods; good disease resistance.

'Sprite' Fast maturing, good cropper, round beans.

'Purple Teepee' Round, purple beans on tall plants. Turn dark green when cooked.

'Cobra' Climbing bean, very reliable and prolific cropper.

'Algarve' Climber, large flat green pods.

'Dutch Brown' Dwarf beans perfect for drying.

'Borlotto Lingua di Fuoco Nano' Climbing drying bean with pretty red and white pods.

RUNNER BEANS

Although commonly known as 'scarlet runners' from their flower colour, some modern varieties such as 'Desiree' have white flowers. If you don't want to put up sticks there are good dwarf varieties like 'Pickwick' and 'Hestia' (which has red and white blooms) to choose from. If tenderness is your goal, then select a stringless bean like 'Polestar' or 'Butler'; if your aim is to win the 'longest bean' class in your annual vegetable show, then grow 'Enorma'. You can also select varieties for early cropping.

Preparation and growing

Runner beans are deep rooted and need good, well-manured soil. Preparation for your runner beans can begin in autumn by digging the 46 cm (18 in) wide trench where you will grow them. If you make it a good 23 cm (9 in) deep you can throw in all kinds of leafy, compostable material from the end of the summer crops and leave it to rot over the winter. Alternatively, dig a slightly shallower trench in spring, about a month to six weeks before you aim to plant your seedlings, and add a good layer of well-rotted manure. If you don't manage to get around to trenching, don't worry. Just dig two good furrows and add manure – either fresh, well rotted or the concentrated kind before planting.

When you are ready to set either seeds or plants, replace the topsoil in the middle of the trench, leaving two straight furrows. The sticks then go on the outside edge, pushed well into the ground to avoid plant roots and to keep them stable in the wind. The sticks for the beans (both runners and climbing French) can go in before or after planting. Plastic clips are quicker to fix than using string or wire. If you want to grow just a few beans up a wigwam, set your plants into generous individual holes, again with plenty of compost. An alternative to sticks is to grow runner beans up sheets of wide plastic or wire mesh which you can roll up in autumn and reuse. It needs to be firmly attached to strong posts placed at intervals of a few feet.

As with French beans, you can plant runner bean seeds direct into the ground, but starting them individually 5 cm (2 in) deep in cells or pots indoors or protected by a frame is much more reliable. Set two at the base of each cane – one each side – but not until after the risk of frosts is definitely over. They will appreciate a foliage feed when first planted, and again after another week or two.

Some pests are particularly partial to runner beans, especially slugs and snails that will even climb the poles. And they will appreciate some extra feed – either as liquid or a top dressing – once pods begin to set. To prevent them getting over straggly, pinch out the tops once they reach pole height. You may need to take step ladders or telescopic loppers to the allotment to do this, or borrow from a neighbour.

top tip

Remember that runner beans are subtropical plants needing plenty of care. Water them well throughout their growing season but don't over water or you will encourage roots to flourish near the soil surface rather than penetrate deep into the soil. If possible, never put cold water onto them at night. Some allotment gardeners sink lengths of perforated pipe into trenches lined with newspaper as a kind of irrigation system.

Allotment Choice

Wind can decimate runner beans by blowing all the blossom off before flowers have a chance to be fertilized. Another way of ensuring good fertilization is to choose them some good companions such as single-flowered dahlias and to select new varieties that are self-fertile.

'Benchmaster' Long, smooth beans.

'Scarlet Emperor' An old variety first introduced in 1633. Still with excellent flavour.

'Kelvedon Marvel' Early maturing; plants medium high.

'White Lady' White flowered heavy cropper. Pods set well in hot weather.

'Firelight' Tolerates hot, dry conditions that can inhibit pod setting. Virtually self-fertile.

'Moonlight' Self-fertile new variety produced by crossing with French beans. Early cropper.

'Stardust' Also a French bean hybrid. Self-fertile white flowers, excellent cropper.

'Sunset' Delicious heritage bean with pale pink flowers. Good drying beans if allowed to mature fully.

PEAS

Eaten straight from the pod, fresh peas are a perfect vegetable so good that once your children discover them you'll find your crop ravaged by human 'pests'. The first, crisp mange touts and sugarsnaps of the season do not quite match up, but are still delicious. (Sugarsnaps are larger and more rounded with developed peas inside but are still eaten whole or raw.) You can also grow tiny petit pois or traditional marrowfat peas which can be eaten fresh or dried to use in soups and casseroles. Other alternatives are asparagus peas (*Lotus tetragonolobus*), aptly named for their taste with deep red flowers and 'winged' pods that are eaten whole.

How to grow peas

To get enough worthwhile 'regular' peas you need several rows. Because of the pressure on space needed by summer and autumn crops, and to have peas early in the year, it pays to get your first sowings of peas done during February – or even overwinter them indoors or protected with fleece, polythene or cloches. They need a well composted soil with good drainage, especially if they are to survive periods of cold and damp, and seeds won't germinate until the soil reaches about 10ºC. Ideally, aim to grow fairly small amounts in succession for second early and maincrops. You will also need to plan on suitable supports, depending on the height of the mature plants.

Peas are best sown in drills about 10 cm (4 in) deep and wide enough to accommodate three rows placed in zigzags with about 5 cm (2 in) between each. Allow 60 cm (2 ft) between parallel drills. If planting in the autumn, sow seeds a little more thickly as you are bound to have some casualties; you can always thin them out later.

Once seeds germinate, thin them only to avoid overcrowding. Be sure they don't get too wet as they can be susceptible to damping off. When they are about 10 cm (4 in) high they will need supporting – left to droop they will be even more vulnerable to slugs and snails. Rather than smooth sticks, they need supports that allow them to cling on with their many tendrils. You can use criss-crossed twigs, lines of string or wire attached at 7.5 to 10 cm (3 to 4 in) intervals between bamboo canes set about 30 cm (1 ft) apart, or netting supported vertically on bamboo poles, making a perimeter around the

top tip

To prevent seeds and young plants being eaten by mice or voles, edge the row with spiky twigs of holly or gorse. Easiest of all is to cover the row with fleece, pegged down firmly and even edged with stones, although success is not guaranteed. An old precaution is to soak seeds in paraffin overnight before you plant them (the odour is a rodent deterrent).

plants. If you live in the country you may be able to buy traditional pea sticks, which will last many years. Otherwise, try improvising. Prunings from garden shrubs and trees, cut canes of autumn raspberries and any sticks you can garner from the allotment boundary all work well.

Keeping plants healthy

Strong plants will need little attention apart from watering. A good mulch put on after a thorough soaking will help keep peas moist. The advantage of early sowings is that they are less likely to be attacked by the pea moth, whose caterpillars hatch inside the pods and consume the contents. Growing garlic nearby can help to deter the adult moths, or you can use an organic garlic spray on the flowers. If you see signs of silver mottling of the leaves and pods, caused by pea thrips, the same spray can also be effective.

Allotment Choice

Peas to choose from include:

MAIN CROP

'Feltham First' Can be overwintered. Makes strong plants.

'Meteor' Shorter, strong plants. Can be overwintered.

'Kelvedon Wonder' Early, good for sowing in succession.

'Early Onward' Heavy cropper, quick maturing

'Jaguar' High yielding second early.

'Hurst Green Shaft' Productive, reliable main crop.

MANGETOUT

'Oregon Sugar Pod' Can be overwintered. Tall plants.

'Delikata' Dark green mangetout pods; long season if cropped regularly. A shelled pea if left to mature.

SUGARSNAP

'Delikett' Dwarf, excellent for windy sites.

'Sugar Lace' Very sweet; plants semi leafless. Good early variety.

'Sugar Ann' Good yield on an early cropper. Also super sweet.

PETITPOIS

'Petit Provencal' Petit pois, early cropper.

MARROWFAT

'Maro' Classic 'mushy' or casserole pea.

BRASSICAS

There is a brassica for every allotment season, but whether you are growing cabbage or kale, Brussels sprouts or broccoli, there are certain conditions that all members of the cabbage family need. Being hungry and thirsty, first and foremost they need fertile soil that has been manured in advance of planting – ideally in the autumn before. Once planted they need plenty of water and regular feeding. They are also fussy about soil acidity, liking a slightly alkaline environment around pH 7.2 to 7.5 (which will also help to deter club root), so you will need to lime the soil in late winter or early spring if necessary.

Brassicas like their roots to be firm; if blown about on a windy site 'root rock' will hinder their growth. If your soil is light, avoid loosening it in spring. You can tread it down if the weather is not too wet.

Many brassicas are best started off in an allotment seedbed or in pots or trays at home. They don't like to be crowded so always sow them thinly or, if you prefer, sow them two or three seeds to a pot or cell. After germination, seedlings will mature more quickly with some protection – either a cold frame or greenhouse if in trays or fleece or polythene on the plot. Once large enough to handle they need to be thinned to about 5 cm (2 in) or potted on. The exceptions are vegetables such as pak choi and Chinese cabbage which dislike being transplanted and are prone to bolting.

top tip

When planting out brassicas, choose a cool day – too much heat will make them wilt irretrievably. Make a hole with a dibber or a slender trowel and pour in some water from a can to 'puddle' them. Set the plant in the hole and firm up the soil all around it with your hands. If you're careful you can also use your heel to make the earth extra firm. Water them in generously and keep them well watered throughout their growing life.

PESTS AND DISEASES

All brassicas are magnets for pigeons, which can decimate them overnight, and for rabbits, so need netting until well established. Slugs and snails are partial to young plants too. Specifically, brassicas are susceptible to some of the most aggravating pests and diseases.

PESTS

APHIDS

Symptoms Plant growth is stunted or even deformed by blackfly, greenfly and whitefly which all do their damage by feeding on the sap of young shoots and leaves. These insects also leave a sticky honey like substance on foliage, making it virtually inedible. In a bad attack just touching a leaf can make clouds of insects fly up; sooty moulds also develop on leaf undersides.

Treatment Spraying plants with a fatty acid preparation works well or make a garlic spray by infusing half a dozen chopped garlic cloves in boiling water for 15 minutes, then straining off and cooling the liquid. If you have a hose on your plot, a thorough wash down can help get rid of aphids as long as you get to the leaf undersides, but be careful – delicate growing tips can be broken off by powerful water jets. Another approach is to buy an organic oil-based treatment which works by impairing the insects' physiology, blocking the pores through which they breathe. Proprietary garlic and pyrethrum sprays (both plants naturally contain large amounts of sulphur) are also effective and safe. If you are growing organically you can buy live ladybird, hoverfly and lacewing larvae and release them to feed greedily on aphids by the hundred.

CATERPILLARS

Symptoms The caterpillars most likely to affect your allotment are those of the cabbage white butterfly. Brassicas of all kinds – and nasturtiums – are their favourite foods. The caterpillars hatch from clusters of green eggs, usually laid on leaf undersides, then munch their way through the foliage. If you see the butterflies flitting round your crops, watch out for the eggs.

Treatment Use fine netting to keep butterflies away. Rub egg clusters off with your hands – a smelly, messy job that demands disposable gloves. Pick caterpillars off by hand and dispose of them. For a bad infestation try a pyrethrum spray. More generally, welcome birds like bluetits to your plot, which consume caterpillars by the hundred. If you have trees on the plot or nearby you may want to put up nesting boxes.

CABBAGE ROOT FLY

Symptoms The maggots of the cabbage root fly attack the roots of newly transplanted brassicas, particularly cabbages and cauliflowers, making them collapse and die. When you pull up the plants you can see the white grubs on the sorry stumps that remain.

Treatment The best way of preventing attacks is to stop the flies laying their eggs at the stem bases. Cover plants with extra fine netting or fleece or make or buy collars to put around the plant bases while they are young and vulnerable. They need to be about 10 cm (4 in) square with a hole in the middle through which you can 'thread' the roots when planting. Cloches or large plastic bottles cut to size will have the same effect.

"Welcome birds like bluetits to your plot, which consume caterpillars by the hundred...."

Symptoms: Pock marked holes in leaves that may then turn yellow.
Treatment Cover plants with fine netting. See also advice for growing rocket and radishes.

DISEASES
CLUB ROOT
Symptoms A soil-borne fungus that causes swollen, deformed roots and yellowed or purplish leaves that quickly wilt in fine weather. Plant growth is poor.
Treatment Because the fungus thrives in acid conditions, lime the soil before you plant. On acid soils add 500 g per sq m (15 oz per sq yard) to achieve the ideal soil pH of around 7 to 7.5. Halve the quantity in future years. Good drainage, helped by adding plenty of compost, will also help. Crop rotation is vital to help reduce the spread. Choose F1 varieties with proven resistance.

WHITE BLISTER
Symptoms White blisters appear on leaves and stems but rarely do serious damage.
Treatment Remove any affected leaves immediately. If stems are badly affected, pull up and destroy whole plants.

Brassicas are also prone to downy mildew (see p 54).

The best ways of cultivating individual brassicas on your allotment feature on the following pages, except for turnips and swedes which are covered in the section on root vegetables, and kohlrabi which is a stem vegetable.

CABBAGE

With good planning you can enjoy allotment cabbage almost all the year round, though in summer you may prefer to give the space to other vegetables. Of all the brassicas, cabbages are among the easiest to grow, but they will still need firm ground that has been well manured, regular feeding and plenty of water through the growing season. Cabbages are easy to grow from seed, planted 2 cm (¾ in) deep, but because they grow quite slowly and often need wide spacing during the prime growing season, sow them in a separate 'seedbed' before moving them to their final growing site. Or sow them in their final positions but thin them as they mature. Avoid sowing too many seeds at one time – instead sow several small batches through spring and summer to spread out your harvests and avoid gluts.

Once cabbage seedlings have four or five good leaves they can be set in their permanent positions, about 45 to 60 cm (18 in to 2 ft) apart in all directions. Discard any that don't have good root

Some popular cabbage choices that should do well:

SPRING
'Durham Elf' Pointed, dark green leaves.
'Pixie' Tried and tested. Very early, small pointed heads.
'April' Withstands tendency to bolt.
'Spring Hero' Compact dark green heads. Earliest with round heads.
'Duncan' Reliable small mid green heads.

SUMMER
'Regency' Pointed heads that stand well.
'Kilaxy' Compact round heads, good club root resistance. Also for late summer.
'Hispi' Summer classic. Fast growing. Good bolting resistance.
'Greyhound' Fast growing, mild flavour.

LATE SUMMER/AUTUMN
'Advantage' Useful for autumn, good all year. Pointed.
'Savoy Perfection' Drum head and crinkled leaves.
'Minicole' Small, round, bright green heads; good space saver.
'Red Jewel' Small firm red hearts.
'Ruby Perfection' Red cabbage, small heads.

WINTER
'January King' Round heads. Will last all winter.
'Marabel' Solid dense heads, reddish outer leaves.
'Tundra' Frost hardy, round heads, will stand all winter.
'Holland Winter White' White cabbage for coleslaw. Cut and keep in November.

systems and plant as deeply as possible. 'Puddle' them with plenty of water, then firm them in well before protecting them from birds and other predators.

Spring cabbages will appreciate some extra treatment. In November, earth up around the plants making a continuous low ridge. This helps to drain surplus water away from the stalks and stabilizes plants against winter winds. In a cold winter, fleece or cloches will give added protection until the weather warms up.

top tip

Pick your planting time for spring cabbages. If planted too late they will be vulnerable to pests, diseases and the winter weather. If planted too early they will bolt if it stays warm through the autumn.

A SOWING SCHEDULE

Spring cabbages Sow in mid to late summer and leave to stand over the winter. Ideally you want plants strong enough by mid-October to survive the winter cold but not so overfed that they mature too quickly.

Summer cabbages, including Savoy and red cabbage Begin sowing seed in February or March, continue to early summer. Transplant in early to late spring.

Autumn cabbages Sow in early to late spring, transplant in late spring to early summer.

Winter cabbages Sow in late spring and transplant in late summer.

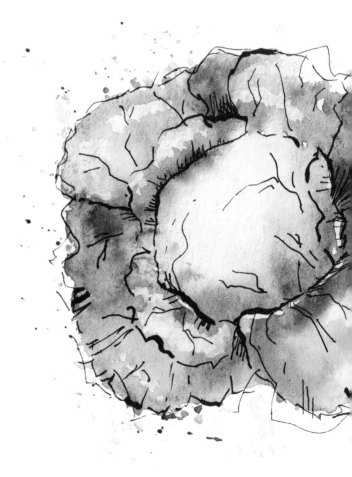

KALE

The hardiest and most disease resistant of all the brassicas, kale is a great winter standby best eaten when the leaves are small and tender. It is a nutritional superfood, packed with calcium, fibre, vitamins and antioxidants. As well as the traditional curly kale, there are newer red varieties to choose from as well as cavolo negro, an Italian kale with slimmer, smoother, dark purplish-green leaves.

Kale seeds, planted in April or May in the same way as cabbages, need plenty of space throughout their growing period if they are to form large, healthy plants. By July they will be ready to plant permanently and will need a good 60 cm (2 ft) between plants in all directions. Although less fussy than some brassicas they need to be firmly set in the ground and, through the winter, firmed in with your foot occasionally. If they seem to be floppy, support them with canes.

Allotment Choice

Kales of serval kinds for a long season:

'Dwarf Green Curled' Heirloom Scottish curly kale dating to 1865. Succulent leaves.

'Kapitan' Densely curled deep green leaves. Exceptionally hardy.

'Redbor' Reddish purple curly leaves.

'Starbor' Dwarf green variety ideal for windy plots.

'KX-1' Bright pink leaves, particularly good when very young.

'Cavolo Negro' Intensely dark green leaves to 'cut and come again'.

"Kale is a nutritional superfood, packed with calcium, fibre, vitamins, and antioxidants...."

BRUSSELS SPROUTS

Sprouts can be tricky to grow, and take up a lot of space, but are well worth the effort if you like them. Most of all they need firm soil – root rock will hinder their growth – plus plenty of food and water. Liming the soil in late winter will release plenty of calcium by spring when plants can be set into the plot. Like other brassicas they need to be netted to ward off pests and kept well watered. As well as the sprouts themselves, the tops make a great vegetable later in the season. Many of the newer varieties have good club root resistance, and look out for purple varieties too.

Raise sprouts like other brassicas, sowing seed in late March or early April and planting them out about 60 cm (2 ft) apart with the same distance between rows. If you put them any closer they will grow small and spindly. Reject any plants

top tip

Plants that rock will often make loose or 'blown' sprouts. Test them by pulling on a leaf. If the plant begins to come out of the ground then it isn't firm enough. If the ground destined for sprouts is clear and not waterlogged during the winter, keep treading on it to harden it up.

without good roots or strong growing points. Plant them quite deeply to help root growth. In a windy plot it helps to stake plants individually, tying them firmly to keep the roots as stable as possible. As they mature or die off, remove the lower leaves to let in light and air.

Allotment Choice

From the dozens of varieties available, some good sprout choices are:

'Crispus' Good club root resistance. Smooth dark green sprouts.

'Igor' Vigorous, reliable heavy cropper.

'Maximus' Early variety with good disease resistance. Smooth dense sprouts.

'Roodnerf' Old Dutch strain. Also good disease resistance.

'Red Ball' Purple sprouts that keep their colour when boiled.

'Clodius' Mid season variety; stands well. Good mildew resistance.

'Long Island' Heritage variety. Semi dwarf with long cropping season.

CALABRESE

Often called and sold as broccoli, calabrese is a quick growing tender brassica that produces central green heads about 15 cm (6 in) across, ready to pick from July to October. Once the central head has been cut, new small ones will grow from side shoots – young leaves are also edible. Seeds can be sown in succession from February to June, and plants treated as for cabbages, but if possible are best sown directly into their final positions and thinned as necessary because they dislike their roots being disturbed. If you do transplant, take care to disturb the roots as little as possible and avoid doing this in warm weather that will encourage bolting. Allow around 45 cm (18 in) between plants. As they mature they will appreciate a water-retaining mulch. It is also helpful to pile soil up around the roots to keep plants stable. Tall varieties may need staking individually. As with all brassicas, crop rotation is vital.

SPROUTING BROCCOLI

Dubbed 'poor man's asparagus', sprouting broccoli is an excellent 'cut and come again' stand by for spring. As well as the traditional purple it also comes in a white variety and there are enough varieties available to give you a harvest from late spring right through to the autumn. Plants are grown like other brassicas but need a generous 60 cm (2 ft) minimum between plants in their final positions. Stake tall plants if they are likely to be affected by wind. Sow seeds in March to harvest in early winter, or from April to mid-June for harvesting from January to May. When allocating space remember that some varieties will need to stay in the ground for almost the entire year.

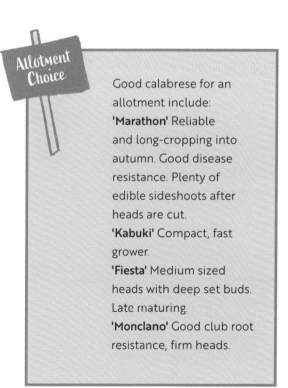

Allotment Choice

Good calabrese for an allotment include:
'Marathon' Reliable and long-cropping into autumn. Good disease resistance. Plenty of edible sideshoots after heads are cut.
'Kabuki' Compact, fast grower.
'Fiesta' Medium sized heads with deep set buds. Late maturing.
'Monclano' Good club root resistance, firm heads.

Broccoli for all seasons. Seed mixtures or blends are excellent value.

WINTER/SPRING

'Early Purple Sprouting Blend' Mix of seeds give plants that mature in succession from late January or February to April.

'Cardinal' Very hardy, crops over a long period.

'White Sprouting' Hardy, crops February or March to April.

'Red Fire' Strong upright plants cropping from January to March.

'Claret' Vigorous heavy cropper.

SUMMER/AUTUMN

'Bordeaux' Purple sprouting, crops July to October.

'Red Admiral' Uniform spears ready to harvest by November.

'Burgundy' Fast growing purple stems.

CHINESE BROCCOLI

For something totally different, with the benefit of being really quick to mature, sow some seeds of Chinese broccoli (Chinese kale) aptly nicknamed 'wok broc'. Although young leaves and buds are also edible as early as three weeks after planting, this oriental vegetable is grown for its thick, succulent tender stems which are delicious when cooked.

The top few inches of the flowering stalks are picked as soon as the flowers appear, which can be as little as a couple of months after sowing. The seed can be sown, either direct or in a seedbed, from early spring to late autumn, then transplanted or thinned to 20 to 25 cm (8 to 10 in) apart. Keep the thinnings for a salad. Full sun is their preference. Slugs and snails love them.

Best varieties include:

'Early Jade' Early maturing; less prone to bolting.

'Kailaan' Thicker, succulent stems and glossy leaves.

'Suiho' Crisp, tender stems and slightly wrinkled leaves.

CAULIFLOWERS

The trickiest of all the brassicas, good cauliflowers are the signatures of allotment 'professionals'. They are particularly intolerant of any form of stress, such as drying out, which will reduce head (curd) growth, a phenomenon known as 'buttoning'. They are also particularly prey to whitefly and caterpillars which will need attention throughout the growing season. As well as traditional white headed cauliflowers there are many new varieties with yellow, purple or lime green heads as in the attractive Italian Romanesco types that look like large pine cones.

Like other brassicas, cauliflowers are bred in varieties that mature in different seasons and, technically, winter cauliflowers are a form of broccoli. Cauliflowers need particularly well prepared soil, which must always be alkaline, and lots of food and water. As with other brassicas root rock will seriously slow their growth. If you use a seed bed on the plot make sure you add some extra peat to the soil and sow the seed sparingly, thinning seedlings to 10 cm (4 in) apart as soon as they are big enough to handle. If you plant them in trays, pot them on. When they have five or six leaves they are ready for permanent planting. Set summer cauliflowers about 60 cm (2 ft) apart in all directions, putting plenty of water in each hole and firming the soil well. Mini varieties will only need 15 cm (6 in) spacing. A top dressing of compost or a high nitrogen liquid feed is helpful at this stage. If you wish, add anti cabbage fly collars until plants are a good size. If the

weather turns cold and dry after you have set out your plants, cover them with some fleece or a cloche to help keep them at a constant temperature.

A SOWING SCHEDULE

Cauliflowers for different seasons need different timings. For cropping in late spring and early summer, sow a variety such as 'Mayflower' under cloches in October, thin them out and keep them protected through the winter before planting out in April. Or sow in a propagator or heated greenhouse in February. Be sure to harden the plants off well before you plant them out.

Autumn Sow late spring/early summer varieties under cloches and overwinter. Generally easier to grow than many other varieties as they mature quickly.

Early spring (or late winter if weather allows) Sow summer cauliflowers, including mini varieties.

Mid to late spring Sow autumn cauliflowers. Will appreciate light shade but best varieties will cope with high summer temperatures.

Late spring to early summer Sow autumn/winter cauliflowers. These mature slowly but produce large heads. Set them well apart.

All you need to do now – though this is not easy in dry summers – is to tend them carefully so that they are never short of water and feed them regularly through the growing season. An additional mulch of compost added after heavy rain or a very thorough watering can help to keep the roots moist later in the season. As the heads – the curds – begin to mature, fold the outer leaves over them to prevent them becoming discoloured or damaged.

top tip

One common reason why cauliflowers fail is a lack of boron. Even if your soil is already alkaline, try mixing 30 g (1 oz) of borax with half a bucket of sharp sand for spreading on an area of 1 sq M (1 sq yard).

Allotment Choice

'All the Year Round' is a great variety for the novice to begin with, and can be sown in any season. Then move on to others such as:

SPRING
'Snowball' Compact, dwarf plants taking up less space.
'Freedom' Highly reliable for an allotment.
'Clipper' Vigorous on water retentive soils.
'Jerome' Super hardy, can be cut in early spring.

SUMMER
'Clapton' Good club root resistance.
'Candid Charm' Large pure white heads and bright green leaves.
'Igloo' Mini variety.
'Raleigh' Good drought resistance.
'Veronica' Excellent Romanesco type.
'Nautilus' Good upright growth, firm heads.

AUTUMN
'Graffiti' Purple heads, vigorous and tolerant of slightly poorer soils.
'Cheddar' As yellow as the cheese; best harvested when small.
'Moby Dick' Crisp white heads. Will tolerate early frosts.
'Sunset' An unusual orange variety; colour most intense in young plants.

WINTER
'Medallion' Large well protected curds.
'Triomphant' The 'Christmas cauliflower'. Can be cropped well into January.

CHINESE CABBAGE

Big, hearty, tight packed green and white heads make Chinese cabbage excellent for stir fries, kimchi and salads but are not the easiest to grow. Unless they have some shade they are quick to bolt and are magnets for both whitefly and slugs. And even the latest varieties are extremely prone to club root. To avoid bolting, seeds are best sown directly into well manured and limed ground (see p30) in May or June, where they will mature quickly if kept well watered. Thin them out to about 15 cm (6 in) apart and enjoy the flavoursome thinnings.

Allotment Choice

Some good varieties to try:
'Yuki' Matures early and relatively disease resistant.
'Natsuki' Slow to bolt. Smooth leaves are thick veined.
'Wa Wa Sai' Quick maturing smaller heads.

PAK CHOI

Quick to mature, pak choi is a rewarding autumn vegetable for the allotment and a perfect stir fry ingredient. The newest varieties have pretty purple foliage. In a crowded plot a good place for it is in the ground occupied by peas or broad beans after they have been harvested. Individual leaves will be ready to pick in five weeks from sowing, mature heads three to five weeks longer. Pak choi is prone to all the usual brassica problems and like Chinese cabbage is quick to bolt, making early and late sowings the most successful. Slugs are particularly partial to it.

Plant seeds in late summer, allowing about 40 cm (15 in) between rows. Put them where they will mature since (as well as heat and drought) they hate being transplanted. They need thinning to about 20 cm (8 in). Being brassicas, they need protection, when young, from flea beetle. An early sowing under fleece in March is a welcome gap filler when there is not much else to pick.

Allotment Choice

Look out for packets of mixed seeds or choose varieties such as these:
'Choko' Slower to bolt in hot weather. Crisp stems and bright green leaves.
'Glacier' Excellent tolerance of hot and cold weather.
'Red Choi' Reddish purple leaves. Tolerates full sun.

MIZUNA AND ORIENTAL GREENS

Like pak choi, mizuna (also called Kyona or potherb mustard), mibuna and komatsuna or mustard spinach are oriental vegetables perfect for stir fries and best grown in the same way. From their increasing popularity, new varieties come quickly to market. All are best planted in early spring or late summer to help reduce their bolting tendencies. Look out, too, for other variations on the theme, some of which have pretty red foliage, and chop suey greens. Oriental seed mixtures are quick and easy to grow and in a warm, wet season will mature in as little as four weeks

Allotment Choice

Look out for mixtures sold under names such as 'Spicy Green Mix', or simply 'Mibuna' or choose varieties such as:

'Kyoto' If protected in winter can be grown all year round.

'Mizuna' White stems and dark green leaves.

'Mizuna Purple' Pale purple stems, great flavour.

"Quick to mature, pak choi is a rewarding autumn vegetable and a perfect stir fry ingredient...."

LEAFY CROPS

All leafy vegetables share a need for plenty of water to prevent them shooting quickly to seed. Swiss chard has the bonus of having edible stems as well as leaves. Spinach and chard are routinely attacked by slugs and snails as well as rabbits and pigeons. You also need to look out for aphids, but these easy to grow vegetables are free of the many pests and diseases that afflict brassicas. The thinnings of all these vegetables can be eaten raw or cooked. Generally, premature yellowing of the leaves is a sign that plants are short of nutrients.

SPINACH

Although quite greedy of space, spinach is reliable, whether you choose the quick growing summer annual preferred by purist cooks, one of the now popular oriental types, or a perpetual variety. Spinach will appreciate some shade if you can supply it. In any event, be prepared for plenty of watering in dry spells. The crop can occasionally be infested with downy mildew. Badly affected plants are best pulled up and destroyed.

Annual spinach

Varieties of summer spinach sown directly into the ground will germinate in days and be ready to pick in a few weeks, so you can sow them between other vegetables like potatoes. They will do even better if the soil is treated with a general fertilizer before planting. Try to plant little and often, scattering seeds thinly in drills about 2.5 cm (1 in) deep and 20 cm (8 in) apart. Early crops, sown from late February or early March are

Allotment Choice

Spinach for a long cropping season:

ANNUAL

'Trumpet' Good mildew resistance.

'Tetona' Slow to bolt. Smooth bright green leaves.

'Mikado' An oriental variety with deep green leaves.

'Medania' Large mid to dark green leaves. Slow to bolt.

'Apollo' Very productive, slow to bolt.

PERPETUAL

'Perpetual' The ever reliable classic. Succession of substantial leaves.

'New Zealand' Substantial leaves on robust, bushy plants.

most useful as they are ready well before the summer staples like beans and peas. Equally, late maturing varieties are great for freezing and enjoying over the winter. A last sowing in August will give you a late crop after most summer vegetables are over and may even survive through to spring and sprout again. Summer spinach needs plenty of water to stop it from running quickly to seed; digging in plenty of compost will help. Look for varieties marketed as being resistant to both bolting and downy mildew.

Perpetual spinach, also known as spinach beet and New Zealand spinach, needs a more permanent position and is best sown in April and again in July. Like summer spinach, rows placed 60-90 cm (2-3 ft) apart are best thinned to leave about 20 cm (8 in) between plants. Longer lived crops will need general, regular feeding.

top tip

A crop for free. If you have the space, leave some summer spinach to go to seed. With luck you'll get a crop of seedlings early in the following spring which can either be thinned out or transplanted to a new position.

"Spinach is reliable, whether you choose the quick-growing summer annual or a perpetual variety...."

SWISS CHARD

Often sold as 'leaf beet', Swiss chard is grown like spinach but it is hardier – and both stems and leaves are tasty. Chard looks pretty in the allotment too, whether you grow the white stemmed sort (confusingly also called sea kale), one of the red-stemmed rhubarb chards or a yellow-stemmed variety. Rainbow chard has multicoloured stems in white, pink, red, orange and yellow. Given well manured ground and plenty of water, seeds sown in May will give you a crop by late summer while second sowings in July or August provide a welcome crop the following April. In mild areas you may be able to pick leaves for the entire year. Chard thrives best if well thinned, so space mature plants about 23 cm (9 in apart), and keep picking the leaves.

Allotment Choice

Chard in many hues:

'Bright Yellow' Striking yellow stems and crinkled leaves.

'Fordhook Giant' Large leaves on strong white stems.

'White Silver' Robust white stemmed choice.

'Charlotte' Striking red stems bearing crinkled leaves.

'Bright Lights' Rainbow mixture with red, yellow and orange stems.

EDIBLE STEMS

The two main allotment crops grown for their stems are asparagus and celery. Florence fennel and kohlrabi are included here too since their edible parts are the swollen stem bases. Although each of these vegetables needs its own special care, give them all good soil and plenty of space and you won't be disappointed.

ASPARAGUS

An allotment asparagus bed will be very productive if you're lucky with the soil and avoid the dreaded asparagus beetle. To have enough asparagus to be worthwhile over its short cropping season you need at least a dozen plants, which will take up a significant amount of space. But the taste of fresh allotment asparagus is so divine that you may think it well worth it. Once established, a good asparagus bed needs relatively little attention and can last 20 years or even longer.

Planning and preparation

It is worth planning for asparagus well in advance. Choose a sunny spot, ideally sheltered from the wind, where there are as few perennial weeds as possible. Certainly, avoid any area where there are horsetails. If your soil is so light that water drains through it in a matter of hours, you may need to take a couple of years to add enough manure to make it suitable for asparagus, or even consider importing topsoil for one or more raised beds.

March and April are the traditional months for planting, so in the late summer and autumn of the year before remove as many perennial weeds as possible and manure the ground well. Heavy clay will benefit from being broken up by the addition of sharp sand. If you select one of varieties now available for autumn planting, manure well in spring and leave the ground uncultivated – except for a few salads – in the months before planting. Male asparagus plants are most convenient to grow as they do

top tip

Keep an eagle eye open for asparagus beetles. The adults of these pests are a vivid reddish yellow and black, though their voracious, greyish larvae are harder to spot. They do not affect the spears, but feast on the leaves and bark of the mature shoots, killing them off and weakening the crowns. Apart from picking off beetles and their dark grey grubs and destroying them, the best remedy for a severe infestation is an organic pyrethrum spray.

not spread seedlings around the plot so check before you buy. Plants can be grown from seed but take an extra year to mature, so ideally order one year old plants (crowns), possibly mixing varieties to extend your cropping season.

PLANTING AND CULTIVATION

Asparagus crowns need to be planted into trenches about 23 cm (9 in) deep and 30 cm (1 ft), wide, set 1 m (3 ft) apart. The base of the trench must be flat enough to spread out the roots of the crowns completely, leaving about 45 cm (18 in) between the tips of each one. Cover them with soil as quickly as you can to prevent them drying out, and water them in. If you wish you can earth them up as the shoots emerge.

When spears emerge, resist cutting them in the first year – and even in the second year, crop them only sparingly. This is essential to allow them to build up crown strength. Keep them well watered and give them a regular twice yearly feed – a mulch of compost in the autumn and a lighter feed, such as a sprinkling of concentrated manure in spring. Although the spears are unbelievably strong, be careful that they are not having to push up through lumps of partially rotted manure. Every autumn, once the leaves and stems have turned yellow, and before composting, cut them down to about 2.5 cm (1 in). Other routine jobs with asparagus are to keep them free of competition from weeds, especially perennial ones. Constant attention will certainly pay off.

Allotment Choice

Try any of these varieties:

'Connover's Colossal' Heirloom variety. A heavy, mid-season cropper and all time favourite.

'Gijnlim F1' Reliable early season green variety.

'Millennium' Green stems with good disease resistance.

'Pacific Purple' Attractive purple stems for a different look. Tender enough to eat raw.

CELERY

Celery comes in two types – self-blanching and trench celery – of which the former needs less attention and is easier to grow, though it is not frost hardy. To do well with either sort of celery you will need well composted well manured soil. You will also need to be able to water your crop frequently. It generally needs a lot of work but worth it if this is a vegetable you favour. Plants are a delight for slugs, especially when young, and it is important to control weeds in the bed.

Seeds of both celery types need starting indoors at a minimum temperature of 10-13°C during March (you can make a later sowing in mid-April for a further crop). When seedlings are large enough to handle, prick them out into trays and, as the weather improves, harden them off. They should be ready to plant out by late May.

At this point, cultivation methods diverge. For self-blanching celery, simply transplant seedlings to the plot, placing them in a block with about 23 cm (9 in) between each. Water them well before you move them and, as you lift them from their tray, try to disturb the roots as little as possible. Water them in well and firm the soil. Keep them well watered and give them an occasional feed until they are ready to harvest in late summer.

In a trench

For trench celery, the tradition is to grow a double row, with plants 23 cm (9 in) apart and with 45 cm (18 in) between rows. In winter, dig a trench 30 cm (1 ft) deep and line it with well rotted

top tip

Both carrot and celery fly will attack young celery plants so you may need to protect them with fine mesh netting or fleece. As a precaution against boron deficiency, which makes celery stems cracked and brown, add borax to the soil before you plant. Be sparing. A tablespoon is enough to treat 17 sq m (20 sq yards) and is best applied mixed with fine sand.

compost. Set established plants in the trench and water them in well. In late summer, cut off any suckers from the base and tie around each plant a double layer of newspaper or black polythene, securing the string firmly. Then use some of the soil from the ridges at the sides of the trench to cover plants to about halfway up their stems. Repeat this earthing up twice more (watering well each time), allowing three to four weeks between each earthing, so that by October just the leafy tops can be seen emerging from the top of a sloping ridge. Dig them as you need them, though it may help to surround them with some straw if very cold frost spells are predicted.

SELF-BLANCHING CELERY

'Loretta' Vigorous grower, stems not 'stringy'.

'Octavius' Succulent stems of medium length.

'Granada' Well flavoured pale green stems.

'Tango' Quick growing, resists bolting.

'Green Sleeves' Greener stems, virtually stringless.

'Blush' Bottoms of stems tinged with pinkish purple. Tasty and colourful addition to any salad.

FOR TRENCHING

'Hopkins Fenlander' Tried and tested old variety.

'Giant Red' Unusual red variety, trenching produces pretty pink stems.

FLORENCE FENNEL

Once you have harvested all your winter cabbages and early spinach and potatoes, use the space for a crop of Florence fennel which has a delicately mild aniseed flavour. Always wait until the weather is warm before you begin. Sow seeds thinly where plants will mature (they dislike being disturbed by transplanting which makes them much more likely to bolt) in drills about 1.25 cm (½ in) deep and about 30 cm (1 ft) apart. As plants mature, gradually thin them to about 15 cm (6 in). Thinnings can be used like the fresh herb. Young plants are particularly favoured by slugs.

top tip

Fennel bulbs will need to be kept well watered or will quickly bolt and set seed, as they will in very hot weather. Warm wet summers suit them best. Otherwise, apart from an occasional liquid feed or top dressing they need little attention. As the bulbs start to form, keep the row well weeded using a hoe to push soil against them to help keep them firm and white.

BEST SELF-BLANCHING FENNEL VARIETIES

'Dragon' Compact round plants, slow to bolt.

'Fennel de Firenze' Large, crisp bulbs.

'Sweet Florence' Traditional old variety, vigorous grower.

'Mammoth' Reliable Italian variety though not as large as its name suggests.

KOHLRABI

The swollen stems that form the edible parts of kohlrabi have a mild taste that is a cross between cabbage and turnip with a hint of pepperiness and can be eaten raw. They are quick to mature and even easier than turnips. They grow above the soil surface and do not mind being transplanted but definitely prefer alkaline soil. Sow seed in small amounts about 1 cm (½ in) deep in succession and in situ from March to July and you should have plants to harvest right through until the autumn frosts. Best harvested when small, they come in purple and pale green varieties (or look for packets of mixed seed) but all have white or pale green flesh. The leaves are also tasty. Being brassicas they have the same issues with pests, especially flea beetle.

top tip

Keep kohlrabi watered well and often. Irregular watering or drying out will make them split and turn woody. They always do best in cooler summers and will appreciate some shade.

"Kohlrabi has a mild taste, a cross between cabbage and turnip...."

Allotment Choice

Some tasty choices:
'Green Delicacy' Pale green skin and pure white flesh with a fine texture.
'Ballot' Purple stems and succulent white flesh.
'Kossack' Large but tender stems.
'Superschmelz' Giant variety with pale green flesh.
'Azur Star' Early; deep purple skin, purple-blue leaves, pale purple flesh.

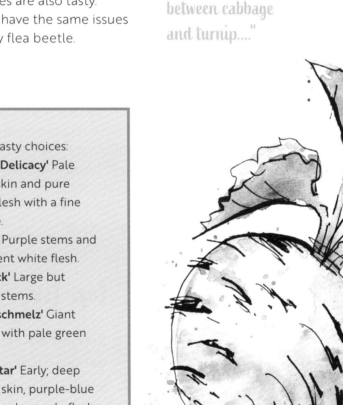

ROOT VEGETABLES

Vegetables that mature underground – which includes here potatoes as well as true root crops like carrots – mostly do well on allotments, though they need plenty of space. They all need fertile, well manured, water retentive soil, but for long rooted carrots and parsnips you need to avoid manuring the soil in the season before planting or you will end up with forked roots if it has not fully rotted down. Most like an alkaline soil, so add lime if necessary. Scattering a concentrated manure or chicken pellets works well for all root crops. Young plants need protecting from slugs and snails, rabbits and similar pests. Those that are brassicas (turnips, radishes and swedes) need protection from flea beetle and cabbage root fly with fleece or fine netting and can be susceptible to club root (see p 66).

RADISHES

There are few finer sensations than the taste of an early radish pulled up, washed under the allotment tap and eaten on the spot. Because they mature quickly – in about four weeks at the height of summer – the rule is to sow seed little and often. Radishes are great space fillers for the gaps around slower growing crops such as cabbages and Brussels sprouts. Seeds of oriental radishes are now widely available and the roots a popular kimchi ingredient.

With fleece or other protection, the first radishes of the year can be sown in late February or early March. Set them in a shallow trench 2.5 cm (1 in) deep and the same distance apart, with 15 cm (6 in) between rows, or put them in a block using similar spacing. Choose traditional or newer varieties, or buy packets of mixed seeds for a variety of shapes and sizes. Above all you need to keep them well watered and pest free.

BIGGER ROOTS

Large rooted mooli radishes are a good crop to put in during June or July, once harvested crops like broad beans allow some extra space. These need thinning to about 15 cm (6 in) apart. They can be harvested before frosts or protected to last through the winter.

top tip

If you sow radish seed too thickly, thin out the crop as it matures. Be meticulous about both thinning and weeding. They dislike being crowded.

Radishes of all sizes to enjoy:

SALAD VARIETIES

'French Breakfast' Elongated shape; an old favourite.

'Scarlet Globe' Round rooted, another all time stalwart.

'Felicia' Elongated roots, good peppery flavour.

'Cherry Belle' Bright red skins and white flesh. Slow to get woody in dry conditions.

'Amethyst' Red-purple skins on globe shaped roots and crunchy flesh.

'Zlata' Yellow skins and white flesh. Good bolt resistance.

LARGER/WINTER TYPES

'Mooli' Long pure white roots. Mild flavour.

'China Rose' Deep pink skins and white flesh. Old variety introduced in 1850.

'Winter Round Black Spanish' Heirloom variety with peppery white flesh.

BEETROOT

If you love beetroot, there is nothing to beat your own crop, whether it's thinnings the size of golf balls or soup made from the last overblown remnants of the crop. And good uncooked beetroot can be hard to find in the supermarket. The spinach like leaves make a great addition to a stir fry.

When sowing beetroot seed, remember that in most varieties (the exceptions are the 'monogram' varieties like 'Solo' or 'Modena') the seeds are actually clusters of three or four seeds fused together, so you need to space them well and be prepared for lots of thinning. Sowing can begin in mid March, if the soil is warm enough, and carry on until July to give you a succession of crops. Set them 2 cm (¾ in) deep and 5 cm (2 in) apart.

top tip

For prize winning beetroot, grow them in a shallow trench about 15 cm (6 in) deep. As they grow, pull the soil over them to keep them red and fresh. This is also helps to keep away hungry mice.

Once seedlings are established, and a couple of true leaves have emerged, you can begin thinning – a job best done after it has rained – leaving the strongest seedling of each group in place. As the plants develop, keep thinning until they are about 10 cm (4 in) apart. Textbook advice is to avoid transplanting them, but it is definitely worth trying, especially if your soil has good water retention. Keep beetroot watered in dry weather, although in good soil it is remarkably drought resistant and generally free of diseases. Plants can be left in the ground all winter, ideally with some fleece to protect them.

Allotment Choice

Select beetroot by their shape and colour. Good ones to try are:

ROUND OR GLOBE

'Boltardy' A justifiably reliable old favourite.

'Red Ace' Very deep red flesh, slow to become woody.

'Globe 2' Has a denser colour and an excellent flavour.

'Barbabietola di Chiogga' Red-orange skin and unusual striped red and yellow flesh.

'Boldor' Sweet yellow flesh beneath copper coloured skin.

'Albina Verduna' Unusual white fleshed variety.

LONG ROOTED

'Cylindrica' Traditional and reliable choice.

'Alto' Super sweet flavour; good space saver.

'Rouge Crapaudine' The 'toad beetroot' cultivated for over 1,000 years and still worth space.

"Keep beetroot watered in dry weather, although in good soil it is remarkably drought resistant...."

CARROTS

There is just no comparison in flavour between home grown carrots and shop bought ones – even those sold as organic. But carrots can be tricky to grow. They are fussy about soil and are plagued by the carrot fly. Even the newest varieties are not immune from infestation. Deep, light loam that drains well is the perfect soil for carrots. Remember that without regular water and feeding, carrots may also show signs of splitting which spoils their looks but not their flavour.

Before choosing from the seed catalogues, which offer carrots in many shapes and colours, decide how much space to allow and whether you want to grow those that will mature both early and late. Ideally, make small sowings of different varieties through the season, right up to August for the latest types. The advantage of very early varieties, which may need protection with fleece, cloches or polythene is that they can be ready

THE DREADED FLY

Carrot fly is hard to avoid, and female carrot flies looking for places to lay their eggs are instantly attracted by the odour released as young plants are thinned out.

SYMPTOMS
· Affected roots are scarred and at worst riddled with tunnels where maggots have excavated their way out.

AVOIDANCE
· If you have raised beds, always use them for carrots. The flies rarely reach more than 45 cm (18 in) from the ground.
· Choose resistant varieties such as 'Maestro', 'Resistafly' and 'Flyaway'.
· Time sowings to avoid attacks (see left and overleaf).
· Try to avoid thinning as much as possible and do it on a dull day or in the evening to minimize the smell.
· Cover plants with fine netting. After thinning do this immediately.
· Alternatively, sow the seed in a block and surround it with a barrier of clear polythene about 60 cm (2 ft) high.
· Apply preparations of nematode worms that will kill off young maggots.
· Plant French marigolds nearby to attract the flies – pretty but not especially effective.

top tip

Sowing carrot seed thinly enough to avoid overcrowding can be tricky. Try mixing the seeds with a handful of soil before you plant them to keep them well separated. However you plant them, be prepared for germination to be slow and mixed.

before the flies attack. Alternatively, seed sown after June 1st is likely to miss the first, strong generation of these pests. Very late sown crops may avoid them altogether. All need to be sown 1 cm (½ in) deep and as thinly as possible in shallow drills about 23 cm (9 in) apart.

Allotment Choice

Some other good carrot choices. Look out for 'Rainbow Mix' seeds for a variety of colours.

'Primo' Early, good for avoiding fly attacks.

'Adelaide' Also early.

'Bangor' Smooth skinned cylindrical roots. Matures in mid season, excellent main crop.

'Sweet Candle' Cylindrical roots, excellent sweet flavour.

'Carruba' Long and pointed, good bolting resistance.

'Autumn King 2' Reliable main crop.

'Chantenay Red Cored 3' Early maturing, good on poorer soils.

'Paris Market' Crops June to October. Stump (round) roots.

'Eskimo' Very frost tolerant. Crops from November to January. Some carrot fly resistance.

'Purple Haze' Vigorous purple skinned roots with bright orange flesh.

'Black Nebula' Deepest dark purple; flesh keeps its colour when cooked.

'Red Samurai' Long roots with bright red skin and pink flesh. Bred in Japan.

CELERIAC

Its beautifully mild flavour makes celeriac a wonderful winter vegetable, but it will do well only on the best of soils, and must have plenty of moisture, so is not ideal for an allotment if you are unable to water very regularly. It also needs a long, unchecked growing season.

To get a good crop, start early in the year, sowing the tiny seeds indoors or in a heated greenhouse in late February or early March – they need a temperature of about 10-13°C. Because they do not like bare-rooted transplanting, they are best sown in deep modules and thinned to one per cell. Once these have three or four good sized leaves (this will take up to five weeks) put them outside to harden off before you plant them out.

Celeriac will not thrive if its growth is severely checked, so you need to be sure that the soil is well composted and as water retentive as possible and free from perennial weeds. Use a dibber or trowel to make a hole for each plant and water into the hole before putting in each plant, placing them about 23 cm (9 in) apart in each direction – they grow well in blocks rather than rows. Make sure that the roots are completely buried and the leaves just resting at soil surface level. From then on it is a matter of food, which should be supplied at two to three-week intervals, water and weeding. A covering of fine mesh or fleece in the early growing stages will help keep celery leaf fly at bay, and give plants a boost of warmth.

top tip

As plants develop – from about August onwards – the outer leaves tend to fall flat. Tear these off (you can use them for flavouring) to let the sun get to the roots. The flavour develops as they get older through the winter. Because celeriac is not frost hardy you need to protect roots if you plan to leave them in the ground all winter. A layer of straw offers good protection, though can be a haven for slugs and snails.

Allotment Choice

Good celeriac choices:
'Monarch' Smooth skins over succulent white roots.
'Prinz' Large white roots slow to bolt.
'Giant Prague' Reliable heirloom variety dating to 1871.
'Ibis' Fast growing with a smooth skin. High disease tolerance.
'Brilliant' Smooth white skin. Flesh slow to discolour once cut.

PARSNIPS

Parsnips are easy to grow on the allotment as long as you can get the seeds to germinate well and avoid canker, the main disease of this crop. Though they take up a considerable amount of room they will last all winter except through the hardest frosts. A fine tilth is perfect for parsnips to prevent them from forking, so don't manure the soil before you sow, but rake in a general fertilizer about a week ahead.

Soil for parsnips should be mildly alkaline (add lime if necessary to correct the pH). Despite what it says on the packet, planting seed in February can be an easy route to failure. Rather, wait until the soil is warm and reasonably dry. A minimum air temperature for good germination is around 12°C (for the soil 7°C), so be patient. Late April and early May sowings are often the most successful. Parsnips are slow to germinate and may rot in the soil if conditions are unfavourable and later planted seeds will soon catch up.

Sow seeds where the crop will mature – parsnips don't react well to being transplanted. After preparing the ground, make a shallow drill, 1 cm (½ in) deep, then water along the base if the soil is dry. Be careful not to sow them too deeply. Scatter the seeds thinly along the drill, or sow three at 15 cm (6 in) intervals. And always sow more than you need – parsnips are easy to thin out to about 20 cm (8 in) apart, allowing about 30 cm (1 ft) between rows. Cover young plants with fleece or fine mesh if you are growing carrots on the plot to avoid fly problems and keep the area weed free, being careful not to damage young roots with your hoe.

With soil rich in organic matter parsnips will only need watering in the very hottest and driest weather. Parsnips can be kept in the ground all winter, and their flavour is said to improve with frost. If it's very icy, cover the tops with fleece or, unless it is likely to be blown away, a thick layer of straw.

top tip

Allotment gardeners have come up with many ways of getting parsnips to germinate, even mixing seed with wallpaper paste (to kill off disease) or germinating them indoors on wet kitchen roll before planting them out individually. Parsnip seed doesn't keep well so always buy fresh each year. F1 hybrids will often be more reliable but also more expensive.

To avoid canker, a fungal disease that turns roots brown or black, with soggy unpleasant flesh, a real problem on heavier soils, choose a canker resistant parsnip variety:

'Gladiator' Reliable F1 hybrid, good canker resistance even in heavy soils.

'Countess' Long roots, white skin and good canker resistance.

'Pearl' Long slim roots last well over the winter.

'Viper' Can produce very large roots, a favourite for showing.

'Picador' Reliable long tapering roots. Good canker resistance.

'White Gem' Less elongated roots but excellent flavour and good canker resistance.

TURNIPS

Turnips are not to everyone's taste, but have become a popular cooks' ingredient, and the latest varieties are bred to produce small, milder roots that are easy to grow and delicious either cooked or raw, when young and tender, after only eight weeks' growing time.

For a supply of young turnips through the summer sow seeds little and often every month, beginning in spring. Very early sowings can be made under polythene or cloches in February, but wait until March to make your first main sowing. Set them about 1.5 cm (½ in) deep allowing around 30 cm (1 ft) between rows. Thin them as they mature and (if you like their rather strong taste) use the tops as 'spring greens'. They should eventually be spaced to about 15 cm (6 in). For a later main crop, sow seed in mid to late summer and leave extra space between plants, around 23 cm (9 in).

Turnip seeds, like parsnips, are sensitive to cold, and will need watering well to prevent the tops bolting and the roots becoming tough and woody. If watered sporadically the roots may split. Because they are brassicas, turnips are susceptible to club root so need to be included in your crop rotation schedule. Liming the soil can help this if it is a problem, and you can also look for seed bred for club root resistance (see overleaf).

Many quick maturing turnips are available in a variety of colours in addition to the traditional main crop:

'Snowball' A round pure white variety good as both a 'baby' turnip and a main crop. Sweet, juicy flesh.

'Aramis' Crimson topped round roots with a nutty flavour. Can be eaten raw. Stands well without getting too large.

'Golden Ball' Golden skin and sweet tasting golden flesh; round roots.

'Sweetball' Quick growing purple-topped roots. Excellent flavour.

'Tokyo Cross' Old hybrid. Quick grower best harvested small.

'Norfolk Purple' Heirloom variety grown since 1680.

'Oasis' Pale yellow roots with a mild flavour. Club root resistant.

'Purple Top Milan' Fast growing flat white roots with purple tops. Good flavour.

SWEDES

Swedes are vegetables for a large allotment, being greedy of space and inexpensive to buy, but have flesh sweeter than turnips, a nutty flavour and are cultivated in essentially the same way. No serving of haggis would be complete without them, and growing them yourself makes it possible to harvest them small and succulent. Being brassicas they are prone to the same diseases but are generally easy to keep in good health Sow seeds in 1.2 cm (½ in) drills in May once the weather warms to give them a good start and to help avoid disease. Thin them as they mature to 23 to 30 cm (9 to 12 in) apart. They are slow to mature but will last well over the winter.

Swedes for the table include:

'Marian' Purple roots and orange yellow flesh. Good resistance to mildew and club root.

'Ruby' Bred for extra sweetness. Dark purple skin and creamy yellow flesh.

'Helenor' Oval roots with a good flavour.

'Magres' Good frost and disease resistance. Yellow flesh.

POTATOES

Just for their fabulous flavour it's worth making the space for a row of new potatoes. Potatoes, like runner beans, are signature allotment crops and will live up to their reputation of helping to clear weeds. However, they do take up a lot of space. You also need to have somewhere to store your crop during the winter unless you plant small quantities.

Potato types

Potatoes come in three main sorts – early, second early and main crop – broadly categorized according to the time they mature. They also vary in the waxiness or flouriness of their flesh, in colour and shape, and in their resistance to attack by scab and other diseases and from wireworm infestation. With a judicious choice of varieties you can have home grown potatoes on your table from early June well into late autumn and even at your Christmas dinner. If you order seed potatoes by mail from one of the big commercial suppliers it is difficult to get small quantities – the minimum is usually 3 kg (6½ lb) which will fill two 5 to 6 m (16 to 19 ft) rows. Look out, though, for 'taster' packs containing 500 g (1 lb) each of three or four different varieties.

Preparation

Ideally, have your earliest seed potatoes ready to chit or sprout by late January or early February. Put them nose end up in cardboard boxes or slatted wooden trays and leave them in a cool, light, airy but frost free place for about six weeks until the sprouts are a good 2.5 cm (1 in) high. Don't put them in the dark or the shoots will be long, weak and straggly. And don't

top tip

Visit local nurseries and buy the exact number of seed potatoes you need. Many will even allow you to buy single seed potatoes to experiment with, such as the fir apples and the purple varieties, relatives of the original potatoes brought from South America.

forget to label them. Meanwhile, prepare the soil in your plot. If you have dug and/ or manured in the previous autumn, you will only need to fork it over to remove the worst of the weeds. Otherwise, add manure as soon as the soil is dry and warm enough to be worked or wait to put it in your trenches.

Planting and care

To plant out potatoes, start by using a spade or hoe to make drills (shallow trenches) about 10 cm (4 in) deep placed about 45 cm (18 in) apart for earlies and about 60 cm (2 ft) apart for maincrop varieties. You can then fill the trenches with compost, shredded paper or leaf mould – anything to improve both food and water retention. As you insert each chitted potato (sprout end uppermost) rub off all but the two strongest sprouts with your thumb. If the potatoes are very large you can also cut them in two at this stage. Use a hoe or rake to cover each completed row drawing the soil up to make a small ridge. When the first shoots

POTATOES GROWN TO SCHEDULE

Use this general guide to planting and harvesting, making allowances for the weather over the season.

Crop type	Planting time	Time to harvest from planting
First early	From end of February	10 weeks
Second early	From mid March	13 weeks
Early maincrop	From late March	15 weeks
Main crop	From late March	20 weeks
Late crop	Late July or early August	11 weeks

appear, cover them with soil – again using the hoe or rake. This will ensure that they are deep enough in the soil but also protect them from any late frosts.

New potatoes for Christmas and the New Year are a possibility with new varieties bred to be planted in July. These late planting (second crop) varieties are, in fact, springtime seed potatoes that have been stored at low temperatures. You can plant them straight into the ground without the need for chitting and they will be ready to lift from late October, or as soon as the foliage is fully grown.

As the season progresses, carry on earthing up until plants are well grown and you have an unbroken line of foliage. Keep an eye open for any potatoes showing above the soil and cover them at once. Light will turn them green and make them inedible. Apart from that there is nothing else you need do except for watering in very dry spells and removing any large weeds that spring up alongside or between your rows. It takes at least 12 weeks for most potato crops to mature. There may even be bonus potatoes. Substandard ones thrown onto a compost heap can sprout to give you an unexpected summer crop.

Potato problems

Blight The most serious of potato diseases. Before the potatoes below ground are mature the leaves,

top tip

If blight strikes, immediately cut the tops off all your potatoes. You will lose some – especially the earlies – but with luck may save the rest. Some gardeners swear by putting rhubarb leaves into the bottom of the trench to prevent it.

years or more before metamorphozing into adults, sow a crop of green manure such as mustard in late summer, adjacent to vulnerable crops. This will not only attract the wireworms but give them sufficient food to speed their maturation in safety.

Eelworms Nematode worms that attack potatoes. Poorly growing plants are found to have cysts the size of pinheads all over them and are liable to rot. There is currently no treatment, but crop rotation is vital to prevent their spread.

Scab Rough, raised patches on potatoes caused by microorganisms that are unsightly rather than deadly. Can be prevented by liming soil well and making sure it doesn't dry out.

attacked by a fungus, become criss-crossed with fungal threads. These are particularly prominent in wet weather, which encourages fungal growth. In the worst cases, the top growth blackens and dies back prematurely and the potatoes rot below ground. When blight is less severe it is possible to save the crop by digging it up as soon as you can. This is also neighbourly. Once spores start blowing around the plot and entering the soil they can affect everyone's crops in subsequent years.

Wireworms A common pest of potatoes –shiny, tough-skinned orange insects, with stiff bodies that protrude from holes in the tubers. These avid tunnellers are the larvae of the click beetle, which lays its eggs in May and June, usually amongst weeds. The best treatment is a nematode preparation applied once the soil temperature reaches 12°C. Because wireworms can live in the ground for four

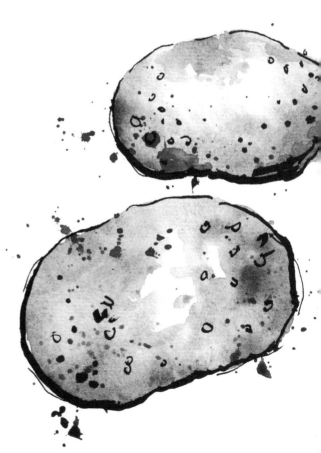

There are dozens of potato varieties – just experiment to find the ones you like best:

FIRST EARLIES

'Rocket' Earliest of all. Soft, waxy white flesh.

'Belle de Fontenay' Pale cream waxy flesh.

'Pentland Javelin' White, waxy flesh. Great for salads; good scab resistance.

'Sharpes Express' Heirloom variety dating to 1900. Floury flesh perfect for roasting.

SECOND EARLIES

'Nadine' High yielding, good disease resistance; white flesh.

'Maris Peer' Creamy flesh that holds its shape when cooked.

'Charlotte' Tender pale yellow flesh; good salad potato.

'Yukon Gold' Traditional Canadian variety, excellent all rounder with a great taste, best of all for roasting. Not always readily available.

'Kestrel' Pale skins with purple splashes. Productive with good disease resistance.

'Vivaldi' Very productive, also works as a main crop. Tubers a pale gold.

MAIN CROP

'Maris Piper' Floury texture perfect for chips.

'Pentland Javelin' White flesh; good all purpose variety. Good scab resistance.

'King Edward' Old classic, cream flesh; a great all rounder. Can also be planted late.

'Desiree' Red skinned; pale yellow flesh. Excellent for roasting.

'Cara' White with pink eyes, white flesh. Ideal for baking; good resistance to blight and eelworm.

'Valor' White skinned, keeps well.

'Setanta' Pink skin and buttery flesh. Great roasters.

'Pink Fir Apple' Knobbly, pink skin, tasty waxy, creamy flesh.

'Annelise Blue' Purple potato. Creamy flesh and a nutty flavour.

LATE CROP

'Rooster' Red skinned, very versatile.

'Carlingford' Waxy, white skinned, versatile.

'Bambino' Slightly waxy flesh. Good scab resistance.

SWEET POTATOES

A warming climate, and the increasing availability of ever more exotic vegetables, has made sweet potatoes a perfectly feasible crop. Unlike ordinary potatoes they are not chitted but raised from sprouted offshoots or 'slips' available to buy. They are best planted in pots of compost to root, then set out as for ordinary potatoes but will only do well in hot summers with high temperatures. They have very decorative climbing stems that can be trained up sticks or left to trail. Usual yield is about five or six tubers per plant.

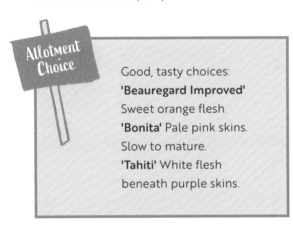

Allotment Choice

Good, tasty choices:
'Beauregard Improved'
Sweet orange flesh.
'Bonita' Pale pink skins.
Slow to mature.
'Tahiti' White flesh
beneath purple skins.

JERUSLAEM ARTICHOKES

The tall shoots of knobbly Jerusalem artichokes make a good border along the side of an allotment, but beware. They are not fussy about soil and reproduce rapidly so can quickly become hard to control allotment 'thugs'. Like potatoes, they are planted as tubers, but do not need to be chitted. Also, they can be left in the ground all winter and harvested as needed. While delicate in taste, they can cause severe flatulence and are fiddly to prepare, so look for smooth skinned varieties.

Plant artichoke tubers about 10 cm (4 in) deep and 30 cm (1 ft) apart then rake up the soil to form a ridge. As the tops emerge and start to grow they can be earthed up some more. Ideally the shoots, which can reach 2 m (6 ft), may need to be tied up to stop them being blown over by the wind or rocking, both of which will bring the tubers to the surface. Metal wire strung between sturdy canes is a good method. To increase tuber size it can help to remove the yellow flowers as they appear. Begin digging them in autumn, after cutting the stems back to about 30 cm (1 ft).

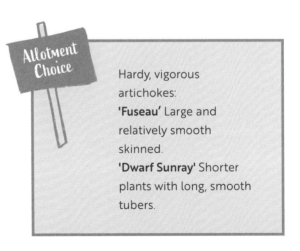

Allotment Choice

Hardy, vigorous
artichokes:
'Fuseau' Large and
relatively smooth
skinned.
'Dwarf Sunray' Shorter
plants with long, smooth
tubers.

THE ONION FAMILY

All members of the onion family – the alliums –are 'greedy feeders' and susceptible to the same diseases. They are most satisfying to grow; properly ripened, dried and stored, onion, shallot and garlic crops will keep you going well into the spring. They need a sunny site and free draining soil high in nutrients.

ONIONS

Although they can be grown from seed onions are really easy to raise from mini bulbs or 'sets' and these are often the best way of reducing the problems caused by pests and diseases. However they are more prone to bolting. Look for those labelled 'heat treated'. Shallow rooted, they need well cultivated, loose soil, ideally not too recently manured, and a sunny spot. If you have the space you may want to grow red and white varieties as well as the 'regulars'.

As long as it is not too cold or wet, onion sets can go into the ground in March. Put them into holes made with a dibber or narrow trowel, set so that the point is just below the soil surface to help prevent birds pulling them up. Set them about 15 cm (6 in) apart. If they push up as they begin to grow (the developing roots can sometimes make them do this) just press them gently back in. Discard any that are soft or show signs of mould. Through the growing season keep onions weeded and watered when necessary, and well fed, either with liquid feed or an occasional top dressing. This is especially important while plants are making leafy growth before the bulbs begin to swell. You can buy a specially formulated onion fertilizer for the purpose.

top tip

For a very early crop you can grow winter onions, planting them in October. However they are unlikely to keep well.

ALLIUM PROBLEMS

There are a variety of pests and diseases that trouble alliums more than any other vegetables. Controlling them can be vital to a successful and plentiful crop.

PESTS

ONION FLY

Symptoms Leaves and bulbs destroyed by fly larvae. Plants are most vulnerable in July.
Treatment Remove and destroy badly affected plants. Try controlling the insects with a nematode preparation. Grow plants from sets rather than seeds.

ALLIUM LEAF MINING FLY

Symptoms Larvae tunnel into the vegetable. Leeks are particularly susceptible.
Treatment Keep plants under fine netting in March and April and again in October and November when they are most susceptible. Destroy badly affected plants.

DISEASES

With all onion diseases take extra care not to spread fungal spores on your hands.

BASAL ROT

Symptoms A fungus that affects any plants growing from bulbs. Leaves yellow and die back and bulbs may rot. If garlic is affected it may not keep well, and even if dried out thoroughly may not last the winter.
Treatment Choose well drained soil for planting and grow onions from sets which tend to be more resistant. Take care not to overwater crops. Be sure to rotate crops. Destroy badly affected bulbs.

WHITE ROT

Symptoms Very similar to those of basal rot, but it attacks more quickly and, in the case of garlic, is more likely to kill the plant outright. If caught early you may be able to remove the most badly affected areas from garlic heads and save some of the cloves, but take care to prevent future attacks. Cool, wet summers pose most risk. Onions and garlic with white rot are unlikely to keep well.
Treatment Avoid planting onions or their relatives in an affected spot for as long as you can – crop rotation is essential. Destroy badly affected plants.

RUST

Symptoms Patches of round bright orange or yellow pustules on plants caused by fungi. Beans and mint can also be attacked. Hot, humid summers are their favourite growing conditions.
Treatment Avoid over fertilizing soil – rusts thrive on nitrogen. When mild needs no attention but for more serious attacks try a sulphur-based fungicide. Avoid over watering. Destroy affected plants and be sure to rotate crops.

See also Diseases p 54.

For good, healthy crops try some of these onions:

'Hylander' Good mildew resistance in a reliable variety.

'Sturon' Medium sized onions. Store well.

'Hybound' Early maturing round variety. Can be grown from seed.

'Sturon' Ever reliable. Stores well over winter.

'Red Baron' Globe shaped red onion with succulent white flesh. Can be grown from seed.

'Paris Silverskin' White globes. Can be harvested when small for pickling.

'Stuttgarter' Yellow skinned variety; popular and reliable.

'Garnet' Reliable red onion.

SPRING ONIONS

'Guardsman' Vigorous traditional variety.

'White Lisbon' Traditional long white stems.

'White Star' Larger white bulbs.

'Furio' Medium sized red variety.

'Lilia' Plump red bulbs.

Growing from seed

Most onions – including pickling or silverskin onions – can be grown from seed planted In puts or pans of seed compost. The advantage of this is that they are more resistant to bolting. Sow overwintering varieties in August, or germinate seed in a warm greenhouse in early January. Seed can be sown directly into the allotment in March. When setting out young plants try grouping them in clusters of about five plants – a technique called multi-sowing which can be remarkably productive – about 25 to 30 cm (10-12 in) apart. This will produce good medium sized bulbs often more welcome in the kitchen than 'monsters', and you can take off individual plants to use as spring onions.

Spring onions

It's good to have a supply of spring onions all year. For early pickings, sow seed in September – plants are hardy enough to survive most winter weather. You can then put more seed under a cloche in February, and make another sowing in May or June. Sow them in shallow drills 1 cm (½ in) deep. With 10 cm (4 in) between rows). If you sow the seed thickly you can pull the thinnings as you need them, but they need spacing out to help prevent downy mildew.

Welsh onions

Also called everlasting onions, these are usually started from young plants set 23 cm (9 in) apart in March and April. They grow into clumps that look like bunches of spring onions and can also be grown from seed. As long as the whole clump isn't gathered, the few remaining onions will continue to produce more stems.

SHALLOTS

Prized by cooks for their mild flavour, and also for pickling, shallots are grown in a similar way to onion sets, but can be put in during February. They need to be planted less deeply – leave the tip of the bulb protruding – setting them 15-20 cm (3-4 in) apart and allowing 30 cm (1 ft) between rows. By July the original single bulb will have multiplied and the tops withered. They can then be lifted out.

Allotment Choice

Shallots for year round taste:
'Camelot' Red skin and white flesh in a globe shaped variety.
'Matador' Reddish brown rounded bulbs. Keep well.
'Longor' A 'banana' elongated shallot. Very productive.
'Zebrune' French heritage variety, banana shape. Can be grown from seed.
'Golden Gourmet' Heavy cropper, excellent flavour.
'Red Sun' Red tinged bulbs with a spicy flavour.

"Most onions – including pickling or silverskin onions – can be grown from seed planted in pots...."

GARLIC

'Plant on the shortest day and harvest on the longest' is the old adage for growing garlic, although in fact late October or early November are much better months for planting, allowing more time for them to establish before the coldest weather sets in. They can also be planted in spring, but they may not do as well. It is best to buy garlic from a specialist supplier or nursery, but it is not impossible to grow it from supermarket heads if you choose those with good, plump cloves. When buying you need to choose softneck types, which have smaller cloves with a mild flavour that mature fast and store well, or stronger tasting hardnecks that are less liable to be affected by winter frosts. You can also grow 'Elephant' garlic, which is not a true garlic but produces huge cloves with a mild flavour. The cloves need to be planted more deeply and farther apart.

Prepare your ground – garlic likes well drained fertile soil – then divide up the garlic heads into individual cloves before placing each about 23 cm (9 in) apart in all directions in rows or blocks. Then use a slim, sharp-pointed trowel to make individual holes into which each can be popped. Make the holes just deep enough that the tip of the clove is still projecting above the ground. Three fat heads will give you about 20 cloves. In spring, when the plants are growing well, garlic will appreciate a top dressing of compost or concentrated manure. At this point you also need to begin to weed regularly, and water in very dry spells.

top tip

As they grow, hardnecks are more likely to bolt, creating 'scapes' – shoots with a bud on the top. Cut them off and use them like garlic in the kitchen. Be sure to use affected plants early on – they won't keep well.

Allotment Choice

A variety of heads:

SOFTNECK

'Germidour' Good sized bulbs with purple skins and a mild flavour.
'Picardy White' Can be planted in spring.
'Rhapsody White' Ideal for an early crop, great flavour.
'Cristo' Pure white bulbs with a pungent flavour.

HARDNECK

'Eden Rose' Traditional French variety, good for storage.
'Czechmate' Compact head with a purple outer skin.
'Lautrec White' French classic with white skinned bulbs.

LEEKS

Hardy and versatile, leeks are a justifiable allotment favourite and economical on space. Choose your varieties according to the stem length and thickness you prefer – or grow some of each. They dislike acid soil, so add lime if necessary before you plant. Leek seeds sown about 1 cm (¾ in) deep can be begun in a seedbed at your plot or at home in containers in February or March. Sow them as thinly as you can, but if they look overcrowded as they germinate, thin them out or pot them on to give you a good selection of healthy seedlings 15- 20 cm (6-8 in) tall. These can then be put into their permanent bed, which needs to have been well manured the previous year.

The traditional way to plant leeks is to make holes about 15 in (6 in) deep with a dibber, trim the top off each plant then put one plant in each hole, fill the holes with water and leave them. However if you need to transplant them when they're smaller, leeks will grow very well planted in deep holes with a trowel or dibber in the normal way. Make sure to use a hoe to earth up all leeks to get the whitest stems. To prevent early

top tip

Leeks will always need plenty of food during their growing season as well as water in dry spells. A midsummer top dressing of concentrated manure is a good idea, as is earthing them up a little with the hoe to produce as much blanched stem as possible.

sowings from bolting, and to help prevent diseases, cover them with fleece or cloches if the weather turns cold.

As well as the usual onion family problems, leeks are prone to rust. If mild, you can just remove affected leaves as you harvest, but badly affected plants may have to be ditched. Don't put these on the compost heap – destroy them safely. The same applies to any plants affected by allium leaf fly, leek moth or onion fly.

Allotment Choice

Leeks with vigour and flavour:

'Musselburgh' Reliable old favourite with for short thick stems.

'Lyon Prizetaker' Long pure white stems. Grown since 1880.

'Pandora' Early variety with long slender stems.

'Toledo' Long stems and dark leaves.

'Oarsman' F1 variety slow to bolt. Little swelling at the base.

'Porbella' Long growing season, stands well over the winter.

VEGETABLE FRUITS

From outsize marrows to superb tasting tomatoes, vegetable fruits are the pride of the allotment. Easy to grow, courgettes are notorious for their fecundity. Most of these vegetables originate in warm, wet climates and need treatment to match, as well as plenty of food and protection from slugs and snails.

It pays to prepare the ground thoroughly, adding loads of organic matter, well before you begin to sow the seeds of these crops. The most tender of vegetable fruits, such as peppers and aubergines, will do well outdoors only in the height of a hot summer and are best grown in a greenhouse or polytunnel. Otherwise, the only serious problem is brown rot, a fungus that turns crops brown after creating a cottony white mould on the stems leaves and fruits. Never compost any infected plant material and always destroy it safely.

COURGETTES

The hardest thing about growing allotment courgettes (zucchini in America and elsewhere) is to control their numbers. It is always tempting to put in an extra plant or two 'just in case' and invariably they all thrive. If this is the case, think about picking the flowers to use in the kitchen as well as harvesting them when really small.

Courgettes come in a range of greens and yellows and some are even striped. You can sow seeds straight into the ground in mid May, but a more reliable method is

Allotment Choice

Some of the many good choices include:

'Zucchini' The reliable classic.

'Defender' Classic heavy cropper. Mid green fruits.

'Tuscany' Dark green fruits on more erect plants.

'Tondo chiaro di Nizza' Oval specked green fruits. Still tasty when large.

'Clarita' Pale green fruits on vigorous plants.

'Parador' Long bright yellow fruits, good flavour.

'Courcourzelle' Striped fruits with a sweet, nutty flavour.

'Squash Balls' Mixture of greens and yellow; round fruits.

top tip

Always plant courgette seeds on their sides. This seems to encourage roots, then shoots, to emerge more easily.

to raise these vegetables indoors in the warmth from late April in pots or, even better, cells. Sow the seeds individually 1.3 cm (½ in) deep, in 7.5 cm (3 in) pots of moist compost. For a later crop, lasting even until November in a mild autumn, sow seeds in June.

When planting out, allow plenty of space – 1 m (3 ft) at least between each – and consider using matting collars or a bark mulch, added after rain, to help water retention if you may not be able to water them frequently. As the season progresses you may find that the leaves become mildewed, but this does not seem to affect the crop. (It is much more damaging to young plants, and can arise if they are over watered.) The most serious problem that can affect courgettes is cucumber mosaic virus, which mottles and stunts leaves and fruits, though most varieties are now bred with good viral resistance. Once the fruits begin to swell feed the plants every 10 to 14 days with a high potassium liquid fertilizer.

MARROWS

Marrows are the quintessential allotment vegetables, but now less popular than courgettes. Their cultivation is essentially same for as courgettes and like them can even be grown on part of the compost heap. Trailing marrows will need at least 1 m (3 ft) to expand in. Once established, they need little attention except for watering, but if you plan to enter 'heaviest marrow' in your local show, nip off smaller fruits to concentrate a plant's energies into one or two super specimens.

Allotment Choice

Marrow plants can trail or be bush like, so your choice may depend on space:

'Bush Baby' Compact bush type. Striped fruits.
'Tiger Cross' Deep green striped fruits; bush type.
'Long Green' Reliable trailer.

SQUASHES AND PUMPKINS

When successful, squashes and pumpkins can achieve giant proportions and quantities, and huge vigour. As well as being great fun to grow many have the great advantage that, if sound, will keep indoors in a cool place all winter. However the smaller 'patty pan' varieties do not keep reliably and need to eaten straight away. Squashes and pumpkins are essentially grown in exactly the same way as marrows and courgettes, and like them need to be set at least 1 m (3 ft) apart. If you are growing just one or two plants you can even put them direct into a pile of compost or on a ridge of topsoil topped with grass cuttings to enjoy

top tip

To stop developing fruit being damaged by pests, or just rotting on the ground, support them on pieces of stone or even small shelves made by putting pieces of wood on top of upturned flowerpots. Stripping away a few of the leaves around each fruit will allow in more sunlight for ripening.

Allotment Choice

Some of the best varieties to cultivate from a wide choice. Winter squashes keep especially well.

SUMMER SQUASHES

'Sunburst' Yellow patty pan squash.

'Harrier' Butternut squash, pale yellow skin.

'Sprinter' Aptly named fast maturing butternut.

'Hasta la Pasta' Spaghetti squash with noodle like flesh.

WINTER SQUASHES

'Sweet Dumpling' Small cream and green striped round fruit. Sweet orange flesh.

'Crown Prince' Large grey-blue slightly flattened fruit. Nutty orange flesh.

'Harlequin' Prolific yellow and green striped acorn shaped fruit. Sweet orange flesh.

PUMPKINS

'Baby Bear' Small, sweet pumpkin.

'Hundredweight' As large as its name suggests. One for competitions.

'Jack of all Trades' Well shaped and perfect for carving.

food, moisture and warmth. Another alternative, for smaller fruited sorts, is to grow them up a trellis strung between poles, as for runner beans.

To get good fruiting, it helps to nip out the tips of the shoots once they are about 45 cm (18 in) long, so stimulating the growth of laterals. If fruit do not seem to be forming well, you may need to assist pollination by transferring pollen from male to female flowers with a paintbrush. The female flowers are the ones with slightly swollen bases.

TOMATOES

When they fruit successfully outdoor allotment tomatoes have a unique taste, so it is always worth planting some, but they can be hit and miss, depending on the weather and the threat of blight. They will also suffer if you cannot get to the plot to water and feed them regularly. If buying ready-grown plants it is important to check on the

variety to be sure that it is suitable for growing outdoors on a plot that may provide little shelter. Many good varieties are now grown as grafted plants to improve their performance and disease resistance and can be ordered from reliable suppliers.

Growing from seed

If you are growing from seed, ideally start outdoor tomato varieties indoors on a windowsill or a heated greenhouse at around 18-21°C any time from mid February to mid April. Sow seeds in good compost and cover them to just 6 mm (¼ in), then keep them warm and moist, though be careful not to over water them as they are prone to damping off. Move them around as need be to stop them growing lopsidedly towards the light.

Once seedlings are large enough to handle, transplant them into individual 7.5 cm (3 in) pots and harden them off. Be careful not to put them into the

top tip

Once fruit start to form tomatoes need feeding every 10 to 14 days. You can buy a commercial preparation or make your own from comfrey or nettles cut and soaked for 1 to 2 weeks in water. The foul-smelling solution needs to be diluted by about 1 in 10 with water.

allotment until plants are good and strong, with five leaves, or when you can see the first signs of flower buds forming. Wait until there is no risk of frost. When you plant, try scooping up the soil around them with both hands, then make a depression all around, so the water runs out, not down and add a little blood and bonemeal. You can also use growing bags at the allotment as long as it's possible to stake them. A bag can work particularly well if cut in half and stood up on its end.

Planting and care

While it is fine to plant tomatoes direct into well composted allotment soil, ideally in a sunny, sheltered spot, it can help to ward off diseases by putting them into deep 19 cm (7½ in) pots, sterilized before filling and either placed on a path or paved area or sunk into the ground. To give them a good start it can help to cover tomato plants with individual bell-shaped cloches They need plenty of water and food, but not in excessive quantities. Help water retention by surrounding the base of each plant with a good mulch; if you are growing them in pots or bags, mix in some 'swell gel' granules to assist with this – or try using it direct in the soil when you plant.

TOMATO PROBLEMS

Watch out for these issues and look out for specifically resistant varieties.

BLIGHT

Symptoms Leaves wither and fruit begins to turn brown, especially in warm, wet weather. Can persist for many years.
Treatment Remove affected leaves. Uproot and destroy affected plants to stop the disease from spreading – minute fungal spores are carried on the wind. Wash your hands thoroughly and treat garden tools with Jeyes Fluid to kill the spores. Rotate crops every year.

BLOSSOM END ROT

Symptoms Ends of fruit become sunken and black, due to calcium deficiency.
Treatment Avoid irregular watering through the fruiting season. Feed regularly.

SPLITTING FRUIT

Symptoms Scar like cracks appear on fruit.
Treatment If possible, avoid letting the soil fluctuate between bone dry and over wet. Keeping plants at an even temperature is desirable but not necessarily possible.

MAGNESIUM DEFICIENCY

Symptoms Lower leaves turn yellow, often caused by over feeding.
Treatment Use a proprietary balanced tomato feed.

Some choices that have a good chance of surviving allotment conditions:

CORDON (INDETERMINATE) TYPES

Need side shoots removing:

'Gardener's Delight' Long trusses of cherry red fruits.

'Consuelo' Cherry type, long clusters of fruit. Good blight resistance.

'Crimson Crush' Large juicy fruit and excellent blight resistance.

'Crimson Plum' Plum tomato with meaty flesh. Good blight resistance.

'Mountain Magic' Medium sized fruit, good blight resistance.

'Moneymaker' Old favourite with medium sized fruit. Available grafted.

'Sweet Million' Favourite heavy cropping cherry tomato.

'Ailsa Craig' First bred in 1908. Deep flavoured red fruit. Reasonable disease resistance.

'Suncherry Premium' Shiny red tomatoes.

'Ildi' Yellow plum tomato.

'Tigerella' Red with orange stripes but not as tasty as some.

'Supersteak' Beefsteak tomato with reasonable blight resistance.

'Indigo Cherry Drops' Purple tomato (semi-bush). Fabulous flavour.

BUSH (DETERMINATE) TYPES

No need to remove side shoots:

'Rubylicious' Small orange red fruits with a tangy flavour. Blight resistance.

'Sungold' Small cherry type. Orange fruits.

'Losetto' Sweet cherry tomatoes. Some blight resistance.

'Summerlast' Very sweet cherry tomatoes. Good blight resistance.

'Black Opal' Near black with a great flavour. A cordon but grow as a bush.

As they grow, tomatoes will need tying to 1.5 m (5 ft) cane supports. Use soft string, not wire, or you will damage the tender stems. On a windy allotment two canes, set opposite each other, are helpful for added support. The other care that tomato plants need depends on the type you are growing. While 'regular' (technically cordon or indeterminate) sorts need their side shoots removing regularly, to leave four to six trusses, with the top shoot taken out to 'stop' the plant once these have formed, bush (determinate) types don't need this treatment.

CUCUMBERS AND GHERKINS

Although they can be quite tricky to get started and established, just three or four healthy plants will give you enough cucumbers to feed a family from July right through until September. There are many interesting cultivars to try, from ridge cucumbers to gherkins.

All cucumber seed needs starting off in pots or cells, either in the warmth indoors in late April – or outdoors in a sunny spot in mid May. Sow single seeds, 1–2cm (½–¾ in) deep set on their sides (to help prevent rotting), in

top tip

Cucumbers will appreciate a general feed, but relish the high nitrogen supplied by regular sprinklings of bonemeal. Rather than letting plants get overlarge and straggly, pinch out the growing tips once you have a good quantity of flowers to encourage growth from side shoots.

Allotment Choice

Full of flavour and good to grow:

'Marketmore' Tried and tested favourite. Great flavour.

'Carmen' Glossy green straight fruit. Good disease resistance.

'Burpless Tasty Green' Easy to grow, mild flavour.

'Crystal Lemon' Unusual yellow skinned round fruits on vigorous plants. Juicy and easy to digest.

GHERKINS

'Cornichon de Paris' Outdoor gherkin. Small prickly fruit great for pickling.

'Venlo Pickling' Productive gherkin, does very well outdoors.

"Just three or four healthy plants will give you enough cucumbers to feed a family...."

individual 10 cm (4 in) pots filled with seed compost mixed with vermiculite (see p 40) and well watered. Because seedlings are very prone to damping off it is vital not to overwater. If disease does strike, then start again in different pots and try more warmth and less water. When problems strike plants can keel over in a matter of hours.

Planting out

Be sure that all frost risk is past before planting out cucumbers in a sunny spot, ideally with some shelter. Mixing soil half and half with spent mushroom compost is one way to give them the nutrients they need. Some gardeners favour planting through a water-retentive membrane, although this can get over hot in high summer. Whatever method you favour, plants need to be about 60 cm (2 ft) apart. Once they start to take off strongly, consider supporting them in some way to save space and to help keep fruit off the ground. Strong wires strung between stakes work well, as does a wicker wigwam. Or you can improvise by growing them, for instance, on an old metal frame.

CUCAMELONS

Not a combination of cucumber and melon but Central American oval grape sized fruits tasting like a mixture of cucumber and lime. They are extremely easy to grow and now readily available as seeds to sow indoors in April and May. Choose a sunny spot and plant them 30-40 cm (12-16 in) apart with canes alongside to support their vines as they grow. Although male and female flowers are borne on the same plant, they are not self-fertile so it is wise to grow several to ensure good fruiting. Once the stems have grown to about 1.5 m (8 ft) pinch out the tops, and do the same for side shoots once they reach 40 cm (16 in). Pick fruit as it matures, from July to September.

top tip

Plants are perennial and will keep over the winter if you dig them up in autumn and keep them in barely moist compost in a shed over the winter before planting them out again in April.

SWEETCORN

Sweetcorn will do well in an allotment provided it has plenty of sun, water and a regular supply of food throughout its growing season. Plants always need to be set in blocks, not rows, to allow the pollen from the male flowers at the top of the plant the best chance of fertilizing the female tassels below. Each plant may not produce more than two ot three cobs, so plan accordingly.

The seeds of sweetcorn need plenty of warmth to germinate but once up will speed away. You can wait until mid May, before you sow seeds direct into the plot or, if you wish, begin them in April indoors. If you do this, enclose each pot in a polythene bag and put them in the airing cupboard until the seeds germinate, then uncover them and transfer them to a sunny windowsill. They need to be set about 2.5 cm (1 in) deep.

Final spacing in the plot needs to be about 30 cm (1 ft) between plants. To concentrate growth into the cobs, nip off any side shoots that appear. The cobs are ready to harvest when the tassels have turned brown and are usually disease free. Squirrels can be a real problem – magpies also find them delicious – so you may well need to make a netting 'cage' to save your crop.

Allotment Choice

The best sweetcorn seeds are marketed under the names Supersweet and Tendersweet which is less chewy. There are also mini varieties:

SUPERSWEET
'Earlibird' Ideal for an allotment. Early to produce sweet cobs.
'Ovation' Mid season variety, large cobs.
'Goldcrest' Tall and vigorous.
'Mirai Gold' Shorter plants, good for a windy site.

TENDERSWEET
'Swift' Quick growing, extremely tasty.
'Lark' Germinates easily; early variety.

MINI
'Mini Pop' Very productive small cobs perfect for stir fries. Harvest just as female tassels begin to show.

GLOBE ARTICHOKES

Tall globe artichoke plants with grey green leaves that are relatives of thistles can make great allotment hedges or dividers, providing some shade or cover in an exposed site. They are an oddity because their edible parts are in fact the 'chokes' or hearts that form the flower bases, plus the swollen bases of the leafy bracts around them.

You can buy globe artichokes ready-grown, but if you prefer to start from seeds these are best begun indoors, above 10ºC then potted on and planted out in well-manured soil in spring, leaving at least 1 m (3 ft) between each. They need well drained soil, plenty of water and a generous spring mulch of compost, though will not usually make globes – unopened flowers – until their second year (and any flowers that form in the first year are best removed to strengthen growth). To maximize the number of heads, cut off small ones as they form and cook and eat them whole, to leave four to six flowers on each plant..

Allotment Choice

Artichokes to choose:
'Green Globe' Large green buds. Not always hardy in colder regions. Heritage variety.
'Gros Vert de Laon' Good hardiness, large green buds.
'Romanesco' Purple tinted flower heads.
'Violetta Chioggia' Italian, also purple tinted. Only hardy in mild regions.

Salads, Herbs & Flowers

For taste, colour and
interest – and lots of quick
easy growing – salads,
herbs and flowers will
brighten up the allotment,
the kitchen and the home.
Experiment to see which
you like best.

SALAD LEAVES

With careful planning it is possible to have allotment salad leaves of some kind almost every week of the year, especially in mild winters, although it pays to protect winter salads such as radicchio with fleece. For most salad vegetables, 'little and often' is the watchword for sowing, since most mature quickly and it is easy to get overrun with excesses. All need well manured soil with good water retention. Equally all are prone to attack by slugs and snails, rabbits and any other animals partial to tasty leaves.

Look out for packets of mixed salad leaves combining, for instance, various lettuces, rocket and corn salad. You can also find Italian salad blends, which will include basil, red-ribbed dandelion and salad bowl lettuce. Mesclun mixes feature lots of spicy flavoured leaves such as 'Koto' spinach, which can also be grown on its own.

LETTUCE

Fresh lettuce all year round is a perfectly reasonable aim for the salad loving allotment gardener. There is an ever-expanding range of textures to choose from – soft butterheads, crispy cos (some of which are described as Romaine), and crispheads. Then there are the loose leaf 'cut come again' varieties particularly good if space is at a premium and you are not able to water as frequently. And colours range from the palest green to deep reds, making them as attractive as they are tasty. Equally, look out for packets of mixed seeds and bolt-resistant varieties.

Indoors, start lettuce seeds off in pots as early as February; they will need the protection of a cold frame, cloche or fleece when you plant them while there is still a risk of frost. By mid March or early April they will germinate readily without additional heat. They also transplant well. Before thinning or transplanting soak the ground with water beforehand, and

top tip

Above all, lettuces need plenty of water. Setting plants quite close together helps water retention, as does keeping them covered with fleece while they establish themselves. Allowed to dry out, lettuces will quickly bolt, though keeping them thoroughly and constantly damp is an added attraction to slugs and snails.

with care afterwards, a technique called puddling. For the very earliest crops, sow seeds of winter hardy varieties in situ August or September and thin them out. Even with some protection you are unlikely to get 100 per cent survival, but you will still enjoy home grown salad early in spring.

Allotment Choice

Get started with – and keep sowing –some of these:

BUTTERHEAD

Soft leaves and open heads to eat fresh:

'Tom Thumb' Compact, reliable old favourite dating to the 1880s. Quick to mature.

'All Year Round' As versatile as its name suggests. Good hearts.

'Clarion' Good heads and disease resistance.

'Diana' Slow to bolt.

'Marvel of Four Seasons' Heritage variety with bronze tipped leaves.

'Valdor' Butterhead winter lettuce.

'Roxy' Red leaved and bolt resistant.

COS LETTUCES

Crisp, oblong leaves:

'Little Gem' Small solid, tasty heads.

'Lobjoits Green' Compact dense heads of larger leaves with great flavour.

'Nymans' Glossy red with softer leaves. Slow to bolt.

'Claremont' Deep green heads. Vigorous and disease resistant.

'Rosedale' Sweet, crunchy head with dark red outer leaves.

'Winter Density' Semi-cos. Tolerant and tasty.

CRISPHEAD

These are iceberg types with round heads:

'Webb's Wonderful' Ever popular, with frilly leaves. Slow to bolt.

'Sioux' Medium sized heads with red-tinted leaves. Good disease resistance.

'Antarctica' Solid heads, good disease resistance.

LOOSE LEAF

'Red Salad Bowl' Frilly leaves tipped in bronze-red. Easy and reliable.

'Catalogna' Flatter green leaves. Lasts well.

'Lollo Rossa' Deep maroon leaves, another good picking lettuce.

'Cardinale' Leaves tipped with red; will also make small hearts.

'Bijou' Purple-red leaves, slow to bolt.

'Black Seeded Simpson' Heritage lettuce dating to the 1800s.
Frilly pale green leaves.

ROCKET

Rocket is expensive to buy and quick and easy to grow. Simplest is annual rocket (*Eruca sativa*), which will even overwinter if sown in autumn and the weather is not too harsh. In late summer it will mature in a month, though in mid season will quickly run to seed. Ideally, sow seeds little and often about 1 cm (½ in) deep and in rows 15 cm (6 in) apart. The seeds are tiny and hard to sow thinly so you need to pull out and eat the thinnings. The flowers, which are very attractive to bees, are also edible.

Wild rocket, (*Diplotaxis tenuifolia*) has a stronger flavour and is a short lived perennial with smaller, darker leaves, that can be picked as you need them. Although it germinates and grows much more slowly than the annual type, don't give up on it. Once established it will readily self-seed.

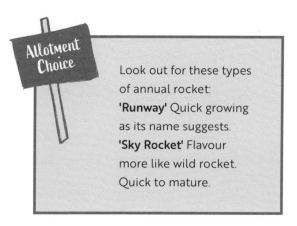

Allotment Choice

Look out for these types of annual rocket:
'Runway' Quick growing as its name suggests.
'Sky Rocket' Flavour more like wild rocket. Quick to mature.

ENDIVE

A quick growing 'cut and come again' salad, endive is a great allotment stand by and less fussy than lettuce. It comes in two types, the robust Batavian or escarole varieties with large, flat leaves or the curly-leaved frisée sorts with loose rosettes of leaves that are slow to wilt in hot weather. They usually have a deeper flavour than lettuce but can be bitter. Plant endive seeds in small batches direct into the ground as you would for lettuce and keep them covered with fleece or a cloche until the risk of frost is passed. They will do best in well composted soil. As you thin them to add to salads, aim for a final spacing of around 25 cm (10 in) between plants.

top tip

Both types of rocket will tolerate less good soil but prefer plenty of water. If you want perfect leaves you will need to protect them from flea beetle, although 'Turkish' rocket is advertised as having some beetle resistance.

Endives in different styles:
'Frenzy' Deep cut very curled deep green leaves.
'Wallone' Robust curly endive; good frost resistance.
'Natacha' Escarole type with a creamy white heart.
'Scarola Verde a Cuore Pieno' Translates as 'green with a full heart' and is a perfect description.

RADICCHIO AND SUGARLOAF CHICORY

Both purple leaved radicchio and its cousin sugarloaf (non-forcing) chicory have a slightly bitter taste that adds depth and bite to any salad. Because seeds are best planted in late summer (to prevent bolting), they follow well in the space left once broad beans or mange tout have been harvested. To help water conservation, and to renew the fertility of the soil, manure the ground well before you sow. In mid season, concentrated manure is good for this.

You can either sow seeds about 1 cm (½ in) deep where plants will mature and thin them out, or sow them in a seed bed and transplant them. For final positioning allow about 23 cm (9 in) between plants. Don't worry if radicchio looks very green when young, As the days begin to shorten in autumn they will redden as the plants begin to heart up. Ideally, they need to be protected from frost with fleece or a cloche to prolong the season. Even in the middle of winter when the outer leaves look mushy you can find good edible hearts within.

A variety of leaves:

RADICCHIO TYPES

'Palla Rossa Bella' A reliably good variety.
'Treviso Early' Dense elongated heads with a sweet flavour.
'Castelfranco' Pale reed leaves dotted with crimson. An Italian favourite.

SUGARLOAF TYPES

'Pan de Zucchero' Good hearts that blanch well.

FORCING CHICORY

Growing forced chicory takes almost a whole year of cultivation, but is worth the effort if you love fresh, crisp winter salads. To achieve the traditional white heads you also need a warm dark place to keep it in while the pale heads or chicons are forming.

To grow chicory at its best – it has long, penetrating roots – you need a reasonably rich soil. Sow it thinly about 1.5 cm (¾ in) deep, direct into the plot, in late spring and thin plants to about 23 cm (9 in). By October or November the leaves will have died down and can be cut off within about 5 cm (2 in) of the base. Dig up the roots, remove any side shoots and trim the tapered ends to leave roots about 20 cm (8 in) long. These now need to be stored in a dark frost-free place. Plant up four at a time to a 20 cm (8 in) pot, cover then with black polythene and bring them indoors. Left in a dark cupboard at about 14°C for three or four weeks they will sprout their chicons which can then be cut off and eaten.

Allotment Choice

For best results:
'Witloof Zoom' Ideal for forcing, good white heads.
'Witloof de Brussels' Easy to grow and forces well.

"Growing forced chicory takes almost a whole year of cultivation, but it is worth the effort...."

SORREL

Common sorrel (*Rumex acetosa*) grows wild in the countryside, producing clumps of highly astringent spinach like leaves that will thrive in almost any allotment soil. However better choices are French or buckler-leaved sorrel (*R. scutatus*) which, being perennial, needs a permanent place. It has a lovely lemony taste. Ideally, sorrel likes some shade, so can thrive under a tree, but whatever its position you need to prevent it from drying out as this makes the leaves taste very bitter. (They also get more bitter as they age.) Alternatively look for red-veined sorrel (*R. sanguinea var sanguineus*) which has long pointed leaves with dark red midribs.

Sorrel seeds germinate best only above 7ºC, so for early pickings they need to be started off indoors in early spring or outdoors once the weather has warmed up. You can begin them in a seed bed and transplant or start them off in situ, but they will eventually need about 30 cm (1 ft) spacing when mature. You should be able to pick young leaves right through the growing season, until plants flower.

CORN SALAD

Also known as lamb's lettuce or, in the French, *machê*, corn salad is a mild, nutty tasting salad and easy to grow. Like rocket it is expensive to buy ready prepared in the supermarket salad section. Look for large leaved varieties like 'Vit' and sow seed as you would for lettuce outside in late summer for autumn and winter salads and in early spring for summer ones. Overwintering plants, though advertised as frost hardy, will appreciate the protection of a cloche or fleece against cold and wet. Because seeds can be slow to germinate, they will do best if you soak them in water overnight before planting them in shallow drills. Otherwise, apart from the ravages of slugs and snails they are trouble free – all they need is some thinning and regular watering.

LAND CRESS

For a peppery taste similar to watercress, land cress (also known as American or winter cress) is easy to grow. Seed can be sown in spring for summer leaves or in autumn to use over the winter. For germination, land cress seeds need plenty of water, so soak the ground well before sowing as you would for lettuce. After germination, thin plants to about 20 cm (8 in) apart.

top tip

Like other herbaceous perennials sorrel is easy to lift and divide in autumn. It will appreciate a good mulch in the spring.

ALLOTMENT HERBS

Herbs at the allotment are especially worthwhile if you have no garden at home. You can make a proper herb garden or scatter your herbs in vacant spaces around the plot – or do some of each. Many are attractive to bees and butterflies as well as adding extra flavour to your cooking. Some, like rosemary, bay and mint will need permanent places, ideally where they will not impede the growth of other plants. To chime with their origins, most need lots of sun. Soft leaved sorts, like basil and parsley, need good protection from slugs and snails. As a rule, the leaves of flowering herbs have the most subtle flavour just before the blooms emerge. After flowering they are much more pungent.

ROSEMARY

A single rosemary (*Salvia rosmarinus*) bush is all you need on the allotment, but you may like a range of varieties. Though not fussy about soil, it will appreciate a sheltered spot, as against the sunny side of a shed, where it will flower in spring and be a magnet for bees. It is easiest to start off with a small plant from a nursery, and once established will grow quickly. Just give it a good cut back once a year after it has flowered. To renew an old rosemary bush, or propagate one, take cuttings of half ripe shoots in summer and keep them in a cold frame or greenhouse over the winter.

top tip

Always look out for 'free' plants. The lower shoots of rosemary will often root themselves into the ground. Cut off, potted up and nurtured over the summer they will make healthy plants.

Allotment Choice

Rosemaries of different shapes:
'Miss Jessop's Upright' Strong blue flowered grower.
'McConnell's Blue' Prostrate grower, blue flowered.
'Majorca Pink' Pale pink flowers on an upright bush.

SAGE

You can grow allotment sage (*Salvia officinalis*) from seed, but it is much quicker and easier to pick up an inexpensive young plant from a nursery or get a cutting from a friend. Ordinary sage has mounds of leaves and pretty blue flowers attractive to bees, but if you use a lot of sage in cooking and want consistent flavour you may prefer a non-flowering variety such as the broad leaved sage sold as 'Culinaria'. Variegated sages are pretty, but not as flavoursome as the regular kind. Other choices include the appropriately named 'Pineapple'.

Sage needs little attention in the allotment and is reliably drought resistant, though it will appreciate a mulch in spring before it starts back into growth (this will also help it produce plenty of foliage). Sage plants get straggly after a few years and will benefit from a good cutting back in autumn, after flowering. It also pays to renew sages now and again. Heeled cuttings, taken during the summer, will root relatively easily in a mixture of potting compost and sharp sand. Overwinter them in a cold frame or greenhouse, or in a cool room indoors.

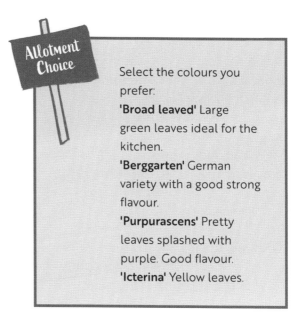

Allotment Choice

Select the colours you prefer:

'Broad leaved' Large green leaves ideal for the kitchen.

'Berggarten' German variety with a good strong flavour.

'Purpurascens' Pretty leaves splashed with purple. Good flavour.

'Icterina' Yellow leaves.

BAY

With a bay (*Laurus nobilis*) on your plot you will have a handsome shrub and a constant supply of aromatic leaves. Be prepared, however, for a plant that outgrows your expectations, and survives against all odds. A small cutting can grow into a tree 10 m (33 ft) tall. As well as the standard species a yellow 'Aureus' variety is available.

All you need for a bay is a sunny spot and secateurs to keep it under control. Small plants are much less expensive than large ones and will quickly establish themselves. To take cuttings in late summer select lateral shoots and remove them with a 'heel'. Inserted into pots filled with equal parts of potting compost and sharp sand, and kept in a frost-free place for the subsequent winter, they should have rooted by spring. It may take another year, at least, however, for them to begin to grow strongly. Once planted out they will appreciate an occasional feed formulated for shrubs.

top tip

Protect young bay plants with fleece in very cold weather.

THYME

If you are growing thyme (Thymus vulgaris) for cooking as well as for its looks, the best choice for the allotment is one of the upright sorts, rather than prostrate or creeping thyme. Thymes look lovely edging a sunny allotment path, and it is worth having several so that you can harvest them freely all year.

Thymes will grow well from seed sown in spring, although they can be slow to get going and, because they are prone to damping off, need to be watered sparingly. Even when established they hate wet winters, so put them in well drained soil where they will get plenty of winter sun. Plants can, however, be unpredictable, not always surviving the winter, especially if it is very wet. If you want to enlarge your thyme collection with cuttings, take them in May or June and root them in a mixture of potting compost and sharp sand.

Allotment Choice

A range of colours and scents: **'Archer's Gold'** Low growing producing mats of lemon scented foliage. **'Fragrantissimus'** Orange-scented, a delight on a summer's day. **'Silver Queen'** Purple-red stems with dark green variegated leaves. **T.citriodorus 'Variegata'** Pale leaves variegated in bluish green and white.

TARRAGON

As long as you can save young growth from being ravaged by slugs and snails, one or two well established plants of tarragon (*Artemisia dracunculus*) will come up year after year to provide you with tasty aromatic leaves. Russian tarragon is much hardier than its French relative, which will be killed by frost, but not a match for it in pure flavour. Buy young plants from a nursery (annually for French tarragon) and put them with your other permanent allotment herbs, ideally in a sunny spot with light well drained soil that has been well manured. To help protect tarragon from winter weather (even the Russian variety dislikes extremes of cold and wet) wait until spring to cut off all the previous year's growth.

top tip

To keep tarragon plants vigorous, dig them up and divide them every two or three years. Do this in spring when they are beginning to grow well.

"Put tarragon with your other permanent allotment herbs, ideally in a sunny spot...."

MINT

Because it can be so invasive, the allotment is an excellent place to grow mint (*Mentha spicata*) also called spearmint, but you will still need to keep it in check. If you don't have a special area designated for herbs, a good place for mint is near the shed, or any other spot that would otherwise be uncultivated. Wherever you decide to put it, you can take your chance on keeping mint confined by digging up and cutting back its spreading roots every autumn or make a 'corral' for the roots with one or more large biscuit tins with plenty of holes pierced in the base. Large drainpipes can work even better. Once it flowers mint is a delight to bees and other pollinators. Ring the changes with some of the many different 'flavours' now on the market.

top tip

Spearmint is particularly susceptible to rust. In case of infection dig out and destroy affected plants and put new plants in a different location.

Allotment Choice

Apart from spearmint there are other good mints to choose from, including:
M. suaveolens Hairy leaved apple mint.
M. x piperita 'Chocolate' Reddish purple leaves with a definite hint of chocolate.

Look out, too, for more unusual, less rampant lime, ginger, orange and pineapple mints.

MARJORAM AND OREGANO

Be careful when you decide to plant either of these closely related perennials that are species of *Origanum*. Once established they can spread everywhere, though make pretty edgings and in flower are a magnet for insects. Of the two, oregano is more robust with a pungent, spicy flavour. Much less tolerant of cold and wet – and less invasive – is sweet marjoram (*O. majorana*), which also has the most aromatic flavour and is often best grown as an annual.

All marjorams need a sunny spot and well drained soil. You can start from seeds or, more conveniently, from small plants. If you see the herb growing around the allotments, ask someone for a few rooted pieces. To keep a good supply of leaves, cut back the flower shoots once they appear, though you may want to leave some plants uncut to attract bees and butterflies. If plants get too big you can simply dig them up and divide them in spring when they are beginning to make new growth.

Allotment Choice

A choice of leaf colours:
Origanum 'French' Hardy plants with a good flavour. Leaves turn golden in summer.
O. vulgare 'Aureum' Pretty golden leaved variety.
O. onites 'Pot' marjoram Bright green leaves and white flowers.

top tip

To grow marjoram from seed, start it indoors, in early March, following the packet instructions. Harden them off before you plant them out. Sweet marjoram cuttings are also easy to strike.

LEMON BALM

Unless you already have it growing on your plot, add lemon balm (*Melissa officinalis*) with caution. The dark green aromatic, lemony leaves are lovely when they first appear but as they flower the plants soon become big and straggly and the leaves tough. The plants quickly spread themselves, and the seeds are incredibly fertile, popping up as weeds all over the plot. It is easiest to keep under control if cut back when coming into flower, but be sure to leave enough for bees to enjoy. Look out for variegated and other attractive forms.

LEMON VERBENA

This lemon scented herb (*Aloysia citrodora*) with purple flowers is a totally different proposition from lemon balm but more problematic as it is a half hardy perennial needing lots of sun that will not survive frost. But it is worth trying for its fabulous flavour and small white or pale purple flowers. One good way of keeping it going is to grow it in a pot that can be taken home over the winter.

LOVAGE

Two or three lovage plants (*Levisticum officinale*) will give you as many tasty leaves as you can deal with – and more. Because they will grow to at least 1.2 m (4 ft) in height, the best place for them is in a corner of the allotment or along its edge. Lovage seeds can be planted in pots in spring or autumn, then transplanted to their permanent positions. Removing the flowers as they appear will give you more leaves. Although it is generally frost hardy, resist cutting lovage right back to ground level in autumn. A little growth left on will afford added protection. If plants get out of hand, dig them up and divide them in spring.

CHIVES AND GARLIC CHIVES

Both 'regular' chives (*Allium schoenoprasum*) and garlic chives (*A. tuberosum*) are simple to grow and pretty in flower – 'regular' chives with purple heads, garlic chives with white ones and flatter leaves. They make an attractive edging but are also useful to help deter pests like carrot fly, which may also influence where you put them. For a more exotic choice, look for flat leaved Siberian garlic or blue chives (*A. nutans*) with bluish purple blooms.

Three good clumps of each sort will provide you with plenty of chives throughout the summer and well into the autumn. Garlic chives, which taste stronger have flat, not rounded leaves, and tend to form smaller clumps. You can grow both sorts from seed or small plants. All will benefit from being dug up and divided into clumps of about a dozen shoots every three years or so, ideally in autumn. If spores of rust are around, chives may be affected. Plenty of water and regular feeding will help make plants resistant, but there is no treatment.

top tip

When the first chives begin to come up in spring dig up a few, pop them in a pot and put them in the kitchen. They quickly shoot up and by the time they are finished the 'main crop' is ready for picking.

PARSLEY

The ubiquitous kitchen herb (*Petroselinum crispum*) is a rewarding allotment grower, though you need to be patient as the seed is slow to germinate. All parsley is biennial, flowering in its second year, so needs to be planted afresh every year to ensure consistent supplies. Whether you choose plain (French) or curly leaved parsley, seeds will need plenty of moisture and, ideally, a consistent temperature to germinate and grow well. An old trick is to pour boiling water on them after planting to speed germination, but in fact this does not make a great deal of difference. They will always take two to four weeks to come through, even with the help of some heat.

Sowing seeds at home in pots or trays – in March for summer crops and July for winter ones – is a good way of getting allotment parsley going, though their roots elongate very quickly and they do not respond well to potting on. On the plot, create deep drills and plant them 1 cm (½ in) deep to allow for root growth. Leave about 30 cm (1 ft) between plants and continue to water them well and keep them fed. As a relative of the carrot, parsley can be prone to attack by carrot root fly, though growing chives, garlic or onions alongside will help to deter these pests.

top tip

Rather than growing parsley from seed buy some ready grown pots from the supermarket and divide them carefully. Choose and plant out those with the best, long roots and protect them from slugs and snails. Plug plants are another good alternative.

Allotment Choice

Parsley old and new in addition to the classic French:
'Moss Curled' The traditional, reliable medium green curly leaved variety.
'Envy' Dark green densely curled leaves in profusion.
'Italian Giant' Flat leaved with a good strong flavour.
'Titan' Robust flat leaved variety.

BASIL

No summer allotment should be without basil (*Ocimum basilicum*), but because it will only thrive when well and truly warm, do not start it off too early. Even if sown outside in May, the warmth of a fleece or a cloche is essential. For a harvest continuing into autumn make one or two more sowings. (To begin them indoors, plant them in modules and keep them at a minimum of 15°C.) When the seedlings are big enough to handle, thin them out and use the thinnings. Keep plants well watered through the summer and early autumn. If the weather is cool they will appreciate continued cover. By July or August you should have plenty of leaves to harvest. Pinching out the tips will encourage fresh growth.

Allotment Choice

As well as 'ordinary' basil many other kinds are both decorative and tasty:

'Genovese' A reliable regular large leaved basil.

'Tuscany' A lettuce leaf or Neapolitan basil with ruffled leaves and a mild flavour.

'Cinnamon' Violet flowers and a distinct cinnamon flavour.

'Purple Opal' Tall purple leaved plants.

'Mrs Burns Lemon' A robust lemon flavoured basil.

'Thyrsiflora' Small leaves with a strong anise flavour.

O. minimum: Greek basil Forms a dense bush with small leaves.

CHERVIL

Although technically a biennial, chervil (*Anthriscus cerefolium*) is best grown as an annual. This hardy herb has a superbly delicate flavour reminiscent of celery. For a continuous crop make two or three sowings 1 cm (½ in) deep through the summer, beginning in March, or when the soil has warmed up; early sowings will benefit from the protection of fleece or a cloche. The last sowing can be in September for winter leaves. Again, protection will help keep these going well.

Once seeds have germinated, thin plants to about 23 cm (9 in) apart. They do not respond well to being transplanted, but you can use the thinnings right away. Chervil likes good drainage, plenty of water and partial shade. Continuous blasts of full sun will make it run quickly to seed. Plants will appreciate a regular feeding as mineral deficiency can turn the leaves brown.

CORIANDER

Like rocket, coriander (*Coriandrum sativum*), also called cilantro or Chinese parsley, is quick to grow and quick to run to seed, but well worth its place in the allotment for its aromatic leaves and spicy seeds. When buying coriander seeds, check whether they are intended primarily for producing leaves (these may be called leaf coriander) or for seeds (often marketed as Moroccan coriander).

Outdoors, coriander needs sowing late to avoid young plants being frosted, and in succession up to early September. It does best in weather that is not too hot and dry and will quickly bolt when the thermometer soars. Thin plants out to about 10 cm (4 in). Plenty of water will help prevent plants bolting too quickly, as will a partly shaded place on the plot and regular picking. Keep it well protected from slugs and snails, especially when young.

Allotment Choice

Some varieties to look out for:
'Leafy Leisure' Lots of good sized leaves. Slow to bolt.
'Cruiser' Large leaves, good bolting resistance.
'Slow Bolt' As useful as its name suggests.
'Lemon' Paler leaves with a citrus note.

DILL

This easy to grow annual (*Anethum graveolens*) with its aniseed flavour needs an open sunny site and enough warmth – an overnight temperature of 7°C or above – to germinate successfully. As with other soft leaved herbs it pays to plant dill little and often for leaves all summer. Dill dislikes being transplanted, so is best sown where it will stay and thinned out a little. Plenty of water and an occasional feed is all it needs. When plants produce their yellow flowers you can pick them whole to flavour pickles or leave plants to go to seed then cut and dry the heads and save the seeds for cooking and planting.

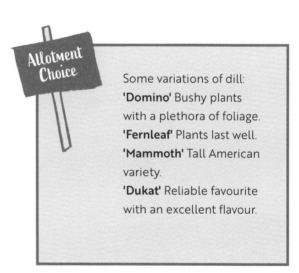

Allotment Choice

Some variations of dill:
'Domino' Bushy plants with a plethora of foliage.
'Fernleaf' Plants last well.
'Mammoth' Tall American variety.
'Dukat' Reliable favourite with an excellent flavour.

FENNEL

Unlike Florence fennel, which is grown as a vegetable, ordinary or common fennel (*Foeniculum vulgare*) is a useful perennial allotment herb. The number and type of plants you grow will depend on whether you are planning to harvest the seeds as well as the leaves. For seeds you may want to choose the attractive bronze leaved fennel ('Purpureum') rather than the soft green type.

Fennel plants are widely available at garden centres and also grow easily from seed sown in spring. Start it in pots and transplant the seedlings or choose a permanent position and thin plants out to about 23 cm (9 in). If you are not going to harvest the seeds, cutting the flower heads down to their base will increase foliage production. For seeds, wait until the heads are just turning brown before snipping them off for drying. When plants die back in autumn, mulch them well. They benefit – in both vigour and flavour – from being divided every three or four years.

BORAGE

With cucumber flavoured leaves essential for Pimm's and other punches, borage (*Borago officinalis*) has the bonus of bright blue flowers beloved of bees. It is a hardy annual easy to grow from seed – you can just scatter them on an area and cover them lightly, and will self-sow in the same spot for years on end.

HORSERADISH

While it is great to have your own supplies of fresh horseradish (*Armoracia rusticana*), think twice before you plant it. Vigorous and invasive, and tolerant of the worst soil, horseradish can quickly take over a large area and is almost impossible to eradicate. If an allotment neighbour has horseradish you may be able to beg or borrow roots (known as thongs) as you need them rather than growing it yourself.

The best way of cultivating – and confining – horseradish is to grow it in pieces of drainpipe about 60 cm (2 ft) long pushed into the ground and filled with a compost and soil mixture. In March pieces of root, ideally 15 to 30 cm (6 to 12 in) long can then be planted into each container and, as they mature, can be used as you need them. Lift the crop in early winter and try to get rid of every bit of root.

> ## top tip
>
> Allowed to spread its seeds unrestrained fennel can easily become an allotment weed, so be careful where you plant it.

ALLOTMENT FLOWERS

The allotment is a wonderful place to grow flowers. They are ideal for cutting and arranging and can often help the health of allotment vegetables by deterring pests and diseases and encouraging pest predators. And many allotment favourites, such as sweet peas and gladioli are flowers that are hard to fit into border schemes at home. But check before you plant. Some allotments place restrictions on the quantity of flowers that can be grown – rules often dating back to wartime. Remember, too, that simpler, single flowers are most friendly to bees and other pollinators. Flat-topped flowers like fennel will also attract hoverflies, also vital to good pollination around the site. As well as the flowers detailed here, try the poached egg plant (*Limnanthes*) and *Cosmos*, both of which are brilliant magnets for pollinators.

EDIBLE FLOWERS

Apart from herb flowers, many of which are edible, including borage, dill, fennel, chive and coriander you may want to grow some courgettes specifically for their tasty blooms. Two other good edible flowers to grow for salads are nasturtiums and marigolds.

Nasturtiums

Vibrant nasturtiums (*Tropaeolum* (*Nasturtium*) *majus*) are guaranteed to brighten any plot and thrive in even the worst of soils. Just sow the seeds 1.5 cm (¾ in) deep and 10 cm (4 in) apart in April and wait for them to mature. They look great on the top of a compost heap and

Allotment Choice

Look for mixtures of nasturtium seeds to give a range of flower colours. Some less usual varieties include:

'Alaska Salmon' Salmon pink flowers with deep orange veins.

'Purple Emperor' Pale purple flowers.

'Black Velvet' Very dark crimson blooms.

'Whirlybird Cream' Pale yellow flowers.

'Chameleon' Pale yellow splotched with crimson.

'Crime Scene' Crinkled deep scarlet petals marked in bright yellow.

set between tomato plants will help to ward off whitefly where you can treat them as 'sacrificial'. If you leave them to self-seed they will come back every year. Look out for caterpillars, which can quickly devastate entire plants. All parts of the plant are edible, including the seeds but the flowers are most often eaten. You can make capers from the seeds (see p 193).

Marigolds

The best marigolds to grow for edible petals are pot marigolds (*Calendula officinalis*). These hardy annuals, with their orange or yellow daisy like flowers, are simple to grow from seed and will thrive in any sunny position and even self-seed. You can wait until late spring and sow seed direct into the plot about 1 cm (½ in) deep or begin them indoors in early spring. Dead head them regularly and you will have flowers for weeks on end. If you plant them near your asparagus they are reputed to help deter attacks by asparagus beetles, but this is certainly not assured!

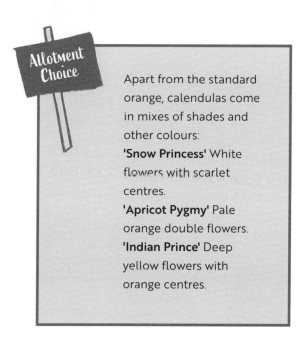

Allotment Choice

Apart from the standard orange, calendulas come in mixes of shades and other colours:
'Snow Princess' White flowers with scarlet centres.
'Apricot Pygmy' Pale orange double flowers.
'Indian Prince' Deep yellow flowers with orange centres.

SWEET PEAS

Grow sweet peas for their gorgeous scent, either in rows, using a double row of canes as you would for runner beans, up wigwams, or against a netting fence. If using canes it will pay to tie string around and between them to create horizontal supports. The seeds, often slow to germinate, are best started in modules indoors (usually in March) and soaked in water for 48 hours or between two pieces of damp kitchen paper ahead of planting to help germination, a process called chitting.

The sweet pea experts sow their seeds in November – with six or seven in a 13 cm (5 in) pot – keeping them in a cold frame or sheltered outdoor spot (and if necessary covered with polythene or fleece) then plant them out in March or April. Sowing them in toilet rolls is another good way to nurture them before planting out. Some gardeners dig deep trenches for them to ensure that the roots stay moist. Whichever method you choose, pinch out the tops of the plants once they have four or five leaves. That way you will get plenty of strong flower-bearing side shoots. Water and feed sweet peas well and keep off weeds and pests. Keep picking them regularly to extend the flowering season and remove pods as they form, except for those you want to keep to sow the following year.

top tip

Sweet pea flowers are attractive to pollen beetles, which lodge inside the enclosed keel petals. An old fashioned way of getting rid of them is to put cut flowers in a yellow bucket. The beetles will fly out, attracted by the colour.

Allotment Choice

There are dozens of varieties to choose from but these should all do well:

'Old Fashioned Scented Mixed' Traditional, prolific heavily scented variety dating to the late 18th century.

'Old Spice Mixed' Heirloom varieties with large blooms and long stems.

'Spencer Mixed' Flowers with slightly frilled petals with long stems. Originally bred by the Spencer family, kin to Princess Diana.

'Fragrant Tumbler' Large well frilled petals in a variety of colours.

AFRICAN AND FRENCH MARIGOLDS

Whether you grow *Tagetes* from seed or buy them as young plants from the nursery or supermarket, these marigolds are bright and cheerful orange and yellow flowered tender annuals that add colour to the allotment right through the season and well into autumn as long as you deadhead them regularly and keep them well watered. Choose from the taller *T. erecta*, the African marigolds, and shorter French types, *T. patula*. To raise plants yourself, sow seeds indoors in March or April then harden them off and plant them outdoors once frost is past. These marigolds can be useful too. Their aroma can help to keep whitefly and other insect pests off crops such as tomatoes, both outdoors and in the greenhouse.

SUNFLOWERS

Ideal for children to grow and measure on the allotment, and great for bees and butterflies, sunflowers are also excellent for cutting and flower arranging. You can also use the seeds to provide food for birds as well as harvesting them for your own enjoyment. Sunflower seeds can be sown under cover in March or April and planted out after frost risk is over, or put straight into the ground in May or early June. Place or thin them to about 60 cm (2 ft) apart. Choose the sunniest spot available and be sure to protect them well from slugs and snails. Rabbits will also devour them. As they shoot up you may need to stake them, as even heavy rain can make them collapse.

Allotment Choice

Sunflowers of different heights. Always check the packet if you're intending to eat the seeds.

'Mammoth' Tall, reaching 1 to 2 m (3 to 6 ft). Edible seeds.

'Giant Yellow' Can reach 2.7 m (9 ft).

'Russian Giant' Tall with huge flowers and edible seeds.

'Teddy Bear' Shorter, reliable variety.

'Lucky Dip' Mixture of sunflowers of different shapes, sizes and colours.

'Suntastic Yellow' Good dwarf variety with long lasting flowers.

DAHLIAS

Tender, thirsty and showy, dahlias flourish on most allotment sites and are excellent for cutting and for show. The simpler flowers also attract useful pollinators. The cultivation season begins in mid March, when you need to start setting stored or newly bought tubers in potting compost, cutting large bunches of tubers into smaller sections to increase your stock. Keep them in a light, frost free place and give them plenty of water until they are well grown (you may need to transfer them to larger pots if they get too big). By late May they will be ready to plant out.

Plant dahlias at a depth of about 15 cm (5 in), with the old stems pointing

top tip

Earwigs love dahlias. To preserve prize specimens, try smearing Vaseline on the stems to stop them in their tracks. Or try putting a pot filled with straw upside down on the top of a cane set among plants. Check every day and empty out the earwigs inside. And remove any you see by hand.

Allotment Choice

Choose some of these for allotment success:

SINGLE FLOWERED

'Bishop of Llandaff' Deep scarlet with golden centres.

'Happy Days' series A variety of colours from pale purple to a stunning pink.

'Anemone' series Flower shapes similar to anemones in many colours.

'Bishop of Dover' Pure white flowers with yellow centres.

'Bright Eyes' Pointed pink petals shading to pale yellow as they reach the flower centre.

OTHER TYPES

Of the thousands available, some easy, showy ones include:

'Jomanda' Long, straight stems and ball-shaped flowers in a beautiful burnt orange.

'Marlene Joy' Spiky flowers with pink tipped white petals.

'Moor Place' A handsome pompom variety with purple blooms.

'Zorro' Giant, decorative purplish-red flowers.

'Baret Joy' White, semi-cactus type.

'Raisers Pride' Medium cactus type with salmon pink flowers.

upwards. To help water retention, it pays to select ground that has been thoroughly composted, and to mulch them well, especially if you are not able to water them every day in dry spells. You also need to protect plants, but especially young ones, from slugs and snails, which relish their juicy foliage. Large plants will also need staking to prevent them being broken by the wind. They need deadheading regularly.

In mild winters, dahlia tubers may survive without being lifted, but are best dug up and removed from the plot once their foliage has died down or been killed by frost. Tubers are prone to disease and need to be kept carefully. Wash them thoroughly, then allow them to dry out upside down, so that moisture can drain from the stem remnants. And don't forget to label them. Ideally pack them with their tops (crowns) exposed in peat or sand. Check them regularly.

GLADIOLI

Gladioli or sword lilies, often hard to fit into traditional borders and wonderful for flower arranging, make first rate allotment flowers especially on free draining soil. They are easy to grow and come in a huge variety of colours and in various shapes, including the pretty butterfly hybrids.

If you plant corms in three or four batches 10-15 cm (4-6 in) deep between mid March and mid April (and a little deeper if your plot is very windy) you should have flowers to cut all summer. For really early blooms sprout the corms in a light, warm spot from mid February, before planting them in well manured soil in rows about 30 cm (1 ft) apart. Putting a little sand in each

top tip

In mild regions gladioli will overwinter, but to be certain, lift and store them over the winter. After the first frosts dig up the corms, trim the tops and put them upside down in a shallow box or tray in a dark, airy place. Be sure to label them. In spring, peel off any shrivelled tissue and break off any small corms (cormlets) before replanting. The cormlets can also be planted, but will not usually flower until their second year.

planting hole will help with drainage on heavier soils. Just keep the slugs and snails off, and give them plenty of water. Should they need extra protection from the wind, insert a stick on the side of each plant facing the prevailing wind and simply tie in the base.

Allotment Choice

Some of the best from a huge range. Look, too, for corms sold in mixtures.

'Byzantius' Brilliant magenta flowers, very hardy, naturalizes easily.

'Nanus' mixture Starlike flowers. Often with cerise marks on the petals. Strong stems.

'Happy Weekend' Large apricot flowers.

'The Bride' Delicate white blooms.

'Impressive' Pale pink flowers splashed with scarlet.

'Vulcano' Deep pinkish red flowers.

'Charm' Purple pink flowers. Good hardiness.

'Miss Green' Tall spikes of white green flowers. Frost tender.

"Gladioli are easy to grow and come in a huge variety of colours...."

ROSES

On a summer evening it is a delight to be able to bring home roses from the allotment. Roses tolerate most soils (though do very well in clay) and also periods of drought, so will survive well without a lot of attention. For best value, buy bare rooted roses by mail order. Most companies deliver between October and March so that plants can be set out whilst still dormant. As long as the roots are kept moist and frost free, they can be stored in their packaging until the

top tip

When planting roses always make sure to avoid damaging the fine hairs at the tips of the roots. To promote root growth, add a scattering of mycorrhizal powder into the hole before you set in the plant.

Allotment Choice

To get best value from allotment roses, good choices are those that repeat flower well into the autumn, old fashioned gallicas, centifolias, albas and musks will do well. Any climbers or rambler will look well over an allotment shed or against a fence or other boundary. Research the possibilities thoroughly before you decide.

ground is workable and reasonably dry. In any event, soaking the roots in a bucket of water for an hour before planting is always a good idea.

Before planting, make up a mixture of one part soil, one part peat and add two handfuls of bonemeal. Then dig a hole large enough to spread the roots out evenly and use your enriched mixture to cover them. Firm this in by treading around the plant. Scatter some manure or mushroom compost around each plant and cover it with a loose layer of soil. If the rose has been grafted, which is most likely, the bud union should be just a little below the soil surface. Container grown roses are also best planted over the winter and, in a dry spell, kept well watered for their first two or three weeks. Aim to disturb them as little as possible. Dig a hole just large enough for the size of the container then ease the plant free and fit it into the hole.

Pruning

As roses bloom, pick them regularly and remove any dead heads to keep them flowering. Leave pruning until spring, then use sharp, clean secateurs to cut out any dead wood or spindly shoots. On healthy branches make sloping cuts, beginning on the side farthest from the bud or eye and slanting towards it, finishing just above the eye. Then feed plants well with a top dressing of compost.

"As roses bloom, pick them regularly and remove any dead heads to keep them flowering...."

Growing Fruit

Fruit bushes and trees,
although greedy of space, are
one of the great bonuses of
an allotment, as long as you
can prevent the birds from
eating your harvest before
you can pick and enjoy it.

SOFT FRUIT

Arguably the best of all, soft fruits are easy to grow provided they are well fed and do not have to compete with a lot of weeds. Get rid of as many perennial weeds as possible before you plant soft fruit of any kind and weed them regularly and carefully. A good way to prepare the ground is as for no-dig gardening (see p 37). Plenty of manure or compost added before planting, and annual mulching, will feed them and improve water retention. For protection, netting will keep off birds, which feed most on early crops. By the time later ones are ripe and ready these visitors seem to have eaten their fill. All soft fruit needs saving from slugs and snails.

STRAWBERRIES

There is nothing quite like the taste of an allotment grown strawberry eaten straight from the plant, but they need some back breaking attention, and plenty of protection from slugs and birds if they are to yield a worthwhile crop. By choosing different varieties (three if you have the space) you can extend the season and avoid gluts.

> ## top tip
>
> If wet weather prompts infection of grey mould, remove affected fruit and destroy it. Don't put in on the compost heap or its spores will persist.

Maximum soil fertility and good water retention are essential for strawberry crops, so dig in plenty of well rotted manure and get rid of as many perennial weeds as possible, or compost before you plant. Increasingly popular is the use of weed suppressing membrane (also available as individual 'mats'). Plants are set through holes made in it. Some of the newest sorts are coated with aluminium foil, which reflects both light and warmth onto the crop. Although they don't look very beautiful they have the added advantage of retaining moisture and keeping slugs at bay, but can make plants overheat in very warm weather.

The strawberry calendar

You can buy plants from good nurseries or online, but if you want specific varieties you may need to order them from specialist suppliers. The strawberry calendar begins in autumn, while the ground is still warm – the best time to start a new bed with bare rooted plants bought in or grown from runners. Set them about 45 cm (18 in) apart, allowing 60-85 cm (2-2½ ft) between rows. Then, in the spring, you can repeat or start the process. In late spring, as soon as flowers are beginning to fade strawberries need to be netted. Traditionally straw was put beneath plants, but you can now by straw matting made specifically for the purpose. They need to be kept well watered and protected from slugs as well as possible. After fruiting, perk up the soil by forking in some compost around the plants. If you wish you can add about 15 g (½ oz) of sulphate of potash per bucketful.

However you grow them, the best way to keep plants vigorous is to replace them every two or three years with new ones raised from the copious runners which appear in late summer. These can be pegged into the soil until established, then moved to the position you want or cut off and raised in pots of compost. To keep established plants vigorous, and to prevent the patch getting crowded out with new plants, snip off all the runners you don't need. In a fine autumn you may even get the bonus of an additional crop.

Allotment Choice

Select strawberries for fruit over a long season. Everbearing varieties will give you several crops in the same year.

EARLY FRUITING
'Christine' Large glossy fruits. Good disease resistance.
'Gariguette' Pointed fruit like large alpine strawberries with a similar taste.
'Mae' Heavy cropper, excellent disease resistance.
'Honeoye' Good choice for cropping and disease resistance.

MID-SEASON
'Royal Sovereign' Reliable old favourite; medium sized fruit. A heritage variety dating to 1892.
'Cambridge Favourite' Traditional and still justifiably popular.
'Pegasus' Very sweet, juicy fruit.
'Hapil' Heavy cropper, tolerant of dry conditions.

LATE FRUITING
'Florence' Easy to grow with firm fruits.
'Rhapsody' Conical fruits with an excellent flavour.
'Symphony' Reliable and tasty semi-evergreen.

EVERBEARERS
'Flamenco' Most productive in early autumn following earlier fruiting.
'Malling Opal' Soft sweet fruit. Survives the winter well.
'Toscana' Will produce sweet fruit for five months.

RASPBERRIES

Allotment raspberries, although they take up considerable space, are a rewarding crop and, if grown from healthy plants, remarkably free of trouble from pests and diseases. By mixing summer and autumn plants you can have fresh fruit almost daily from June to October.

Because they are shallow rooted all raspberries crave well manured soil and minimal competition from perennial weeds. They also like plenty of sun and, if possible, shelter from the wind. The summer sorts, especially, need to be provided with supports to prevent roots from rocking and stems from snapping. If you have just a few plants you can use a series of canes, but a whole row is best supported with a line of posts between which is strung wires at different heights, the top one at about 1.7 m (5 ft) from the ground. As shoots grow, tie them in with plastic ties or strong string.

The best way to begin with all raspberries is to set bare rooted plants into the ground in November or March in a manured trench about 7.5 cm (3 in) deep, and about 45 cm (18 in) apart.

PERFECT TIMING

The treatment that raspberries need depends on when they fruit and on which type of growth.

SUMMER RASPBERRIES

These fruit on wood formed in the previous year. For strong, healthy plants, don't let summer raspberries fruit in the first year after planting. When shoots come into flower, cut the tops off them before they have a chance to fruit. In subsequent years, cut back canes that have fruited and are beginning to die back to a few inches from the ground in the autumn and prune any straggly tops from new canes. Keep summer raspberries under netting to protect the fruit from birds.

AUTUMN RASPBERRIES

These raspberries fruit on new shoots which begin to start into growth in spring. Once these have fruited, leave the canes in place until early spring, then cut them all back to about 10 cm (4 in). Because healthy plants will spread rapidly you may find new plants sprouting all over the place in spring. Dig up those you don't want before your patch gets overcrowded. If you want to renew old plants (they should last a decade or more), pot up these spares and grow them on so that you can make replacements in the autumn. Autumn raspberries are rarely troubled by birds so don't usually need netting but perennial weeds such as convolvulus, which twines up the canes, can be a nuisance. Adventurous snails will also climb to enjoy the fruit.

After planting, cut the canes to about 5 cm (2 in) above soil level to discourage weak, twiggy growth and encourage good root systems. Every spring, take out any weeds as they appear and give all your raspberries a good mulch which will help water retention and help disease prevention. You can use manure, bark or other woody debris which will also feed them, ideally re-creating the acid conditions of the woodlands in which they thrive in the wild.

"By mixing summer and autumn plants you can have fresh fruit almost daily from June to October...."

top tip

After cutting back autumn raspberries keep the most sturdy canes – they make good pea sticks.

Allotment Choice

Select varieties for months of fruit:

SUMMER

'Glen Moy' Early heavy cropper with spine free stems.
'Tulameen' Delicious fruit, good mould resistance.
'Glen Ample' Heavy cropper on spine free plants. Good disease resistance.
'Malling Jewel' Early to mid season, great flavour.
'Octavia' Large berries ready in late summer.

AUTUMN

'Autumn Bliss' Large fruit on sturdy canes. A tried and trusted favourite.
'All Gold' Sweet bright yellow berries.
'Polka' Strong canes and succulent fruit.
'Joan J' Delicious fruit on spine free canes.
'Polka' Very large fruit; a Polish variety.

GOOSEBERRIES

If gooseberries are fruit you favour, make room for at least one bush on your allotment. There are different colours to choose from and some are sweet enough to be eaten raw as a dessert fruit. When selecting new plants – they are best bought two or three years old – it pays to choose varieties with good mildew resistance. Bare rooted plants are best planted in autumn, but container grown bushes can be added at any time. Set them 1.2-1.5 m (4-5 ft) apart into well manured soil, ideally in a sheltered part of the plot. Keep them well watered and in early spring feed them with a general fertilizer rich in potassium and add a good layer of water retaining mulch.

Annual pruning will keep gooseberries healthy and fruiting well. Your aim should be to keep plants nice and open. In winter (and well before March), cut back current season's shoots to about half their length, and cut away any branches that are crossing. As fruit forms cut stems back to five leaves beyond the

top tip

Protect gooseberries with netting in winter to prevent birds from damaging the buds. You may also need it in summer to keep them away.

maturing fruit to let in sunshine and make fruit easier to pick. Always be sure to wear gloves and keep your arms well covered. New plants grow readily from cuttings and low branches may even root themselves to do the job for you. As well as mildew, the other common problem with gooseberries is the gooseberry sawfly, whose caterpillars can quickly strip a plant of its leaves. If you act in time, removing the offenders by hand is the best solution. Even if all the leaves have disappeared you can still get a reasonable crop.

Allotment Choice

Fruit for cooking and eating raw:
'Invicta' High yielding green favourite with good mildew resistance.
'Greenfinch' Lots of green fruit and less spiny than most.
'Hinnonmaki Green' Sweet green berries, good mildew resistance.
'Whinham's Industry' Delicious red dessert fruit.
'Leveller' Large yellow dessert berries with a great flavour.
'Captivator' Deep red dessert fruit, nearly thornless and good mildew resistance.

BLACKCURRANTS

The distinctive scent of blackcurrants is one of the great allotment pleasures. Because blackcurrants freeze so well, and make excellent jam, it is worth growing several bushes if you have room. Blackcurrants are also easy to propagate from cuttings, so you can always expand your collection later. The newest cultivars are bred to be resistant to mildew and in those such as 'Ben Hope', the fruits in each bunch (strig) all ripen at the same time. They are also resistant to bud mite. Plant out bushes in the autumn or winter, allowing about 1.75 m (6 ft) between each, into soil that has been weeded and thoroughly composted. To strengthen young bushes, cut them down to about 2.5 cm (1 in) after planting. It will be worth sacrificing the first year's crop.

Routine tasks with blackcurrants are making sure that they are well mulched in both spring and autumn and keeping them pruned, cutting out old wood to keep the centre of each bush open and uncrowded. Because blackcurrants fruit on strong, young wood, this is best

top tip

To take blackcurrant cuttings, in October snip off pieces of the current year's growth, trim off the soft tip of each one just above a bud and place the cuttings in a small trench in a corner of the plot into which you have put some sharp sand. Within a year they should be well rooted and ready to transplant.

done in early autumn. Netting is essential – birds devour blackcurrants – but if you're protecting bushes individually, remember to allow room for the bush to grow and make sure it is easy to take off and on when you want to pick the fruit. The one pest to avoid is blackcurrant big bud mite, which makes the buds swell, and even drop off. You should always pick these off and destroy them as soon as they appear.

Allotment Choice

Select one of these varieties bred for good health:
'Ben Connan' Large berries on compact plants resistant to mildew and bud mite.
'Ben Lomond' Flowers late in spring so likely to avoid frost damage. Excellent in colder areas with high yields.
'Ben Sarek' Smaller, compact plants with very large, sweet berries.
'Ebony' Super sweet fruit best eaten raw; can lose its flavour when cooked.

RED AND WHITE CURRANTS

Just one or two redcurrant bushes will give you plenty of fruit for sauces and jellies and to freeze for dishes like summer pudding. Cultivation of these fruit is generally as for blackcurrants. However they need pruning differently because they fruit on old wood and at the base of new ones. This is best done in February, making cuts back to strong buds and shortening each branch by about half. In early summer, as fruit is forming, cut back new growth to five leaves beyond the highest sprigs to let in air. As plants mature, cut out some old wood from the centre if it is making the bush congested.

Gall bud mites may attack redcurrants as well as black ones, and redcurrants are also susceptible to coral spot, a fungus characterized by red cushion-like lumps on the wood of the plant. Any shoots that show such disease should be cut out and destroyed.

Allotment Choice

Currants in two colours:

RED

'Rovada' Late summer cropper with large fruits.

'Red Lake' Harvest of dark red fruits in mid summer.

'Stanza' Excellent quality fruit in mid season.

WHITE

'Blanka' Reliable heavy cropper.

'White Grape' Large, sweet berries

BLACKBERRIES AND HYBRID FRUIT

Blackberries thrive on allotments and often grow wild around allotment edges and paths for all to pick and enjoy. Cultivated varieties will, however, give you bigger, juicer berries, and may have the practical advantage of being thornless, but think carefully about where to put them. If you have fencing around your perimeter, additional supports plus horizontal wires will allow you to train them relatively easily. For space saving, try an upright variety such as 'Loch Tay'. To avoid problems later, put supports in place before you begin. Plant out cultivated types at any time from November to March. Apart from an annual mulch, and pruning of fruited stems to ground level, they need very little care and are more likely to be a problem if they spread by self-rooting their long stems.

Blackberries with and without thorns:

PRICKLY

'Ashton Cross' Best flavour of all varieties.

'Black Beauté' Sweet fragrant berries, few thorns.

THORNLESS

'Loch Ness' Self supporting early fruiter.

'Waldo' Early fruit on sturdy plants.

'Merton Thornless' Excellent flavour; plants of medium size.

'Chester' Late ripening heavy cropper.

'Adrienne' Firm, sweet berries from late July.

Tasty hybrids

You can grow loganberries, boysenberries, tayberries in the same way as blackberries, though all need plenty of space. All yield well in a sunny spot, although loganberries are not fond of chalk. For ease of handling both branches and fruit, look for the latest thornless varieties.

Hybrids are often sold without varietal names, but look out for these:

LOGANBERRIES

'LY 654' Large juicy berries with an excellent flavour on thornless stems.

TAYBERRIES

'Medana' Large reddish purple sweet fruits. Bred in Scotland.

'Buckingham' Thornless with large berries.

BLUEBERRIES

As well as tasty fruit, blueberries will give you bee friendly flowers and wonderful autumn colour. Unless you have extremely acid soil of a pH 4.5 to 5.5 you'll only be able to grow blueberries in big pots or a raised bed, or in a confined area filled with ericaceous compost. If you choose pots, select those that will withstand frost – blueberries won't fruit unless they are exposed to winter cold. Plant young bushes in winter, from November to March and, critically, add a generous annual mulch of sawdust, thin wood chippings (shreddings) or leaf mould to boost the acidity. Avoid using manure or mushroom compost that will probably be alkaline. As fruit ripens pick it regularly to enjoy it at its best.

Apart from needing plenty of sunshine and water, and a yearly feed in spring, ideally with an ericaceous fertilizer, blueberries need little other attention apart from netting, but will appreciate a twice yearly addition of a slow release blood, fish and bone fertilizer to keep nitrogen levels high. Prune off any low branches that touch the soil and, annually, any dead wood. Because the fruit is borne on the tips of the previous season's growth, late in the year you need to prune in winter, taking back about a third of the branches on a mature bush. They also need to be kept moist.

Allotment Choice

These should do well in an open plot:
'Bluecrop' Strong plants with flavourful berries.
'Northland' Hardy with small but juicy fruit.
'Spartan' Very good flavour and autumn colour.

"As well as tasty fruit, blueberries will give you bee friendly flowers...."

CAPE GOOSEBERRIES (PHYSALIS)

Expensive to buy, the stunning looking edible fruits of *Physalis peruviana* are annuals, easy to grow in a sunny place as long as you can keep them from being eaten by slugs, snails and rabbits and give them lots of water. Cape gooseberry seeds need to be germinated in the warmth – ideally under glass at 18-21°C and planted out in May or June about 60 cm (2 ft) apart. 'Regular' species plants will grow up to 2 m (6 ft) but there are also good dwarf varieties such as 'Little Lantern', which are generally sturdier. Once flowers have been fertilized and fruits are beginning to form, keep the plants fed with a general fertilizer (tomato fertilizer is fine). They are ready to eat when the fruits have turned orange and the husks are crisp and papery.

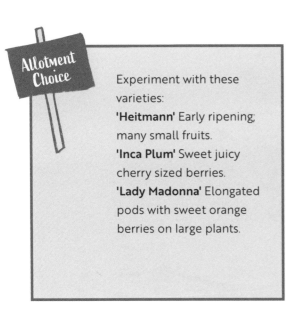

Allotment Choice

Experiment with these varieties:
'Heitmann' Early ripening; many small fruits.
'Inca Plum' Sweet juicy cherry sized berries.
'Lady Madonna' Elongated pods with sweet orange berries on large plants.

RHUBARB

Technically a vegetable, but grown as a fruit in a sunny spot, just one or two good rhubarb crowns in fertile well composted soil will give you more than enough to feed a family. An allotment corner is a good place for rhubarb, provided it has enough room to expand. Both autumn and early spring – as long as the ground is not frozen – are good times for planting rhubarb crowns and true to their reputation they thrive on soil enriched with plenty of organic matter. Don't plant the crowns too deeply; the new shoots should be above the surface of the ground, and resist harvesting the first year after planting.

top tip

For an extra early crop, cover the crown with straw or bracken over the winter, then in late January or early February put an upturned bucket, old drainpipe (or a proper rhubarb forcer) over the plant to encourage slim, tender new shoots.

Year to year, keep your rhubarb well watered and mulched. Pull or cut out any flowers as soon as they appear and put them in the compost to prevent weakening plants, and resist harvesting after about July. If a clump becomes overcrowded, lift it completely and divide it, discarding the old woody parts. Then choose healthy, younger growth to make new plants.

Allotment Choice

Rhubarb for a long season:

'Timperley Early' Ideal for forcing and ready as early as February.

'Grandad's Favourite' Another very early choice.

'Red Champagne' Long, sweet red stems. An old and reliable favourite.

'Victoria' Green, sweet non-stringy stems.

'Fulton's Strawberry Surprise' Red stems in mid season. Does not need forcing.

'Stein's Champagne' Mid to late season, good flavour.

'Goliath' Aptly named for its productivity. Mid to late cropper, can be forced.

TREE FRUIT

Fruit trees can do well on an allotment if you have the space – and as long as trees are allowed. But there are snags, not least because picking and pruning a large tree can be difficult away from home. Also, trees create shade which can be a help, but they will sap a great deal of water from the surrounding soil. If you are lucky enough to inherit an existing tree in good condition it is worth working to keep it healthy. Or you may want to try reviving existing but neglected trees rather than have them cut down or taken out. Never let fruit trees compromise your safety.

APPLES

An apple tree or two can add greatly to a plot, and you may acquire trees with your allotment. These could well be grown from pips rather than being grafted and bear poor quality fruit. While some are self-fertile, others will need pollination from nearby trees.

Old trees

Before you decide to try renovating an old tree, wait to see whether it produces any fruit. To discover its variety, try matching it with illustrations in books or on websites, or look out for 'apple days' at your local nursery. In winter, when a decent tree is dormant, begin by cutting out as much dead wood as possible and any branches that cross each other to achieve a nice, open centre. If the branches are too thick to respond to loppers they will need to be sawn through, for which you will almost certainly need tall ladders and, for safety, someone to hold them for you.
If your apple is a 'bush' type (which won't produce fruit buds at the tips of

> ## top tip
>
> Once the tree is in good shape, keep it that way by pruning every winter. There is no need to paint over the cut ends of the branches, but a pruned tree will appreciate some feeding. Rather than spreading compost around the base, dig a series of holes about 23 cm (9 in) deep, fill them with manure and water them in well. The same goes for established trees you've planted yourself.

the branches), cut back excess growth from the top of the tree if you can. If branches are long and smooth, reduce the tops of these by about a third. If it is a spur-producing apple (with short, rather knobbly side shoots that grow

from the branches) cut back both the branch tops and any large side shoots. Should you be lucky enough to inherit a 'Bramley' or 'Worcester Pearmain', both of which produce fruit near the tips of their branches, thin out the tree centre. If you need to, just take the tops of branch leaders to a good looking bud, but avoid lopping off tips of the lateral shoots.

New trees

Starting from scratch, decide whether you need or have space for two or even three trees or whether a single one will do. Look around and see how neighbours' trees are doing. Two pollinators will be essential unless your apples are self-fertile. A Bramley will need at least two other varieties as pollinators. What's essential is to know which pollinating group (A, B, or C) the apple of your choice belongs to. To get fruit you need matches from the same group. The advantage of beginning with young trees is that as well as giving you the choice of your favourite varieties, you should be assured of healthy stock. You can also keep trees in shape by pruning a little each year. A nicely compact variety will help avoid the dangers of annual climbing exploits.

An apple is best planted at any time between November and March when the soil is workable and wet. Modern varieties are grafted onto rootstocks of different sizes. A semi-dwarf, grafted onto an M9 rootstock is compact and easy to pick from, or you can choose a dwarf rootstock M27. Ask your nursery for advice before you buy or check carefully on expected size, especially if buying plants online.

top tip

If conditions are favourable, clusters of apples will begin to form by late spring. Some will drop naturally, but if it is easy to get to the fruit thin them out by hand. Use clean scissors or small secateurs to cut off any damaged, blemished or misshapen fruit and space the remainder to about 15 cm (6 in). Repeat the operation about two weeks later. Later, if any branches get too heavy, you may need to prop them up with some kind of forked support.

From a huge range, decide whether you want to grow cookers, eaters or those that are dual purpose. And be sure to check on their demands for fertilization before you buy.

SELF-FERTILE

'Herefordshire Russet' New eater with excellent flavour.

'Red Windsor' Crisp dessert apple. Pick from September.

'Greensleeves' Dessert apple, heavy cropper, turns from green to gold when ripe from late September.

'Scrumptious' Crisp, strawberry flavour. Ripe from late August.

'Charles Ross' Dual purpose, crisp and tangy, ripe from October. Does even better with a pollinator.

'Annie Elizabeth' Heritage cooking apple dating to the 1850s. Ready in October stores well. Even better with a pollinator.

APPLES NEEDING POLLINATORS

'Bramley's Seedling' The ultimate heritage cooking apple from the 1850s. Fluffy texture and great flavour when cooked. Needs two other pollinators.

'Worcester Pearmain' Sweet, strawberry flavoured flesh. Ripe from Mid September, but not the best keeper.

'Lord Lambourne' Reliable mid season dessert apple, crisp and juicy.

'James Grieve' Dual purpose early season apple, excellent flavour.

'Fiesta' Easy to grow late season dessert apple. Stores well.

'Golden Noble' Fruits on young trees. Popular heritage cooking apple.

Planting step by step

Before planting, soak the roots in a bucket of water to which you have added a spadeful of compost and leave them for at least an hour. Dig a hole about 50 cm (20 in) deep and wide enough to accommodate the tree roots when well spread, then add a little compost. Drive in a supporting stake alongside the hole, ideally covered with a plastic guard, then put in the tree with its 'neck' – the join between the top growth (the scion) and the rootstock – at least 7.5 cm (3 in) above the level of the soil. Fill in with soil and water well, then use a plastic or rubber tie to attach it firmly to the stake. It may help to add a watering spike alongside so that you can, if need be, water straight down to the roots. If you're planting more than one tree, allow a generous 4.5 m (15 ft) between them at least.

Apple problems

Attack by the caterpillars (larvae) of the codling moth are the cause of maggoty apples, rotten inside. The moths lay their eggs in the young fruit, then feed from within as it matures, making it drop prematurely. To help reduce attacks, hang up a pheromone moth trap in early May. In its base put a sticky sheet followed by a pheromone pellet which exudes a scent similar to that of virgin females, luring and trapping male moths and preventing mating. For additional protection, in autumn tie wide strips of greaseproof paper around trunks and paint on fruit tree grease that will stop females in their tracks.

Canker is a disease that affects apple tree bark. Cracks with raised edges form in the branches from which a whitish gum may ooze. The best remedy is to cut away any affected branches and to cover the cuts with a proprietary wound sealant to prevent further infection.

top tip

An old remedy for maggot problems is to tie strips of corrugated cardboard, smooth side outwards onto the trunk in July. Mature larvae will crawl down the trunk and be trapped inside, where they will hibernate. In early spring you can simply remove and destroy the cardboard. Every winter, to help keep problems at bay, give apples an annual wash with a mild disinfectant. Dilute the concentrate bought at a nursery as instructed and spray it liberally on as many branches as you can.

PLUMS, GAGES AND DAMSONS

These stone fruits are the stars of the allotment (gages are simply less hardy forms of plum). They are not too big, and are reasonably quick to mature – you should get fruit within three or four years. Even if not self-fertile, most plums pollinate easily, so you should be able to get a good crop from just one tree. Modern plums are grown on semi-dwarfing VVA-1 rootstocks so that trees are a reasonable size, even when mature. Damsons, close relatives of plums, are also easy to grow but not as sweet. However they are excellent cooked or made into jam, jelly, chutney or a fruit syrup.

For the allotment, choose a sheltered spot that is going to suffer least from frost and wind as blossom can be decimated in cold, windy springs. Autumn is the best time for planting – follow the same directions as for planting an apple, placing trees about 3 m (10 ft) apart, and keep young trees well watered. They will appreciate a mulch of compost in the first couple of years to help keep the roots moist, but subsequently need feeding only every two or three years. Over feeding will stimulate plants to produce stems and leaves rather than fruit. As trees mature the only pruning they need is to cut them back lightly to keep them in shape. Do this in late summer, before they become dormant, to help avoid silver leaf infection.

Plum problems

Silver leaf, a fungal infection that makes the leaves turn silver, is the most common problem with plums. When severe it also affects the bark, which may even have patches of the purple fungus on them. The best treatment is to cut away any affected branches and destroy them. And be sure to disinfect any tools you've used to save spreading the spores. A very badly infected tree is best removed altogether. Codling moth caterpillars like plums as much as apples, so deter and trap them in the same way.

top tip

It is important to prevent branches laden with fruit from breaking, as wounds can be entry points for disease. Thinning a heavy crop is advisable, but should not be done before the end of June, after the tree has dropped excess fruit naturally.

Allotment Choice

The pick of plums and gages:

PLUMS

'Victoria' Ever popular dessert variety dating to 1844. Ready in late August.

'Czar' Firm, purple skinned cooking plum, good partner for 'Victoria'. Ready from mid September.

'Opal' Ready from early July, Large fruits with yellow flesh.

'Haganta' Large blue cooking plums. Heavy cropper in late season.

'Warwickshire Drooper' Dual purpose yellow self-fertile plums. Good cold resistance.

'Marjorie's Seedling' Late flowering, deep purple fruit best for cooking. Harvest from mid September.

GAGES

'Cambridge' Yellow-green fruit, ideal pollinator is 'Marjorie's Seedling'. Ready from mid September.

'Imperial Gage' Self-fertile, green fruit, good for colder areas. Harvest from mid August.

'Oullins Gage' Large yellow skinned fruit with an excellent flavour. Self-fertile.

DAMSONS

'Merryweather' The most easily available variety. Self-fertile.

'Aylesbury Prune' Sweeter round fruit, ready late in the season.

CHERRIES

A cherry tree is fine for the allotment as long as you can pick and enjoy the fruit before the birds do. It will prefer a well composted, well drained and slightly acid soil with good depth. There are two types of cherry, the sweet ones (*Prunus avium*), some of which are self-fertile, and the acid types that are always self-fertile (*P. cerasus*). Both are best bought grafted onto Gisela 5 rootstocks which restrict the growth to a height of 3-4 m (10-13 ft). Plant trees as for apples and mulch them every spring with a good quality manure to help water retention and provide essential nitrogen. In late winter they will appreciate a general fertilizer rich in potassium such as a fish, blood and bonemeal preparation.

Protection for cherry trees is vital. If spring frost threatens, try covering a small tree with fleece at night to prevent damage to the blossom, but be sure to remove it during the day to allow bees ready access. Fleece – or netting – is also good to keep off birds. A fruit cage is best of all. Once the fruit has been harvested, prune trees of their oldest wood, which will help remove the threat of silver leaf disease and cankers. Remember that acid cherries bear their fruit on the previous year's growth which needs to be kept in good shape.

Allotment Choice

Reliable cherries to enjoy:

SWEET CHERRIES

'Stella' Black cherry, heavy crop ripens in late summer. Self-fertile.

'Sweetheart' Many red fruits over a longish period in late summer. Self-fertile.

'Kordia' Mid summer sweet cherry with large black fruits. Not self-fertile.

'Merchant' Early summer harvest of dark red fruit. Not self-fertile.

ACID CHERRIES

'Morello' Originally brought by the Romans. Juicy red fleshed fruit in late summer.

PEARS

Almost all the advice that applies to apples is also right for pears. Pear trees do grow on allotments, and can be huge on old sites where trees are many decades old, but are worth keeping only if fruitful and healthy. A good choice for a new tree would be a self-fertile variety grown on a dwarf rootstock such as Quince Eline or Quince C, but most pears will only reach their full potential if cross pollinated with another tree and can take many years to produce fruit.. The biggest problem with pears is often wind, which can blow off the blossom before it has been fertilized and sweep bees and other pollinators off course. If your plot is sheltered by a hedge or wall then you are likely to have more success.

Pears will appreciate an annual mulch of good compost in early spring as well as a thinning of any fruit you are able to reach during June. Earlier in the year small trees may need fleece protection as for cherries. They need pruning in winter to keep trees well open and encourage fruiting.

Allotment Choice

Some of the best choices:
'Beurre Hardy' Heritage variety dating to 1858. Melting flesh tasting of rosewater. Good disease resistance.
'Conference' Reliable favourite, good for cooler regions. Good keeper.
'Beth' Small, sweet fruit on compact trees.
'Concorde' Heavy cropper, elongated fruits with an excellent flavour. Reasonably compact.
'Joséphine de Malines' Pinkish white, juicy flesh. Excellent keeper.

Allotment Harvest

After all the efforts of digging, planting, weeding and watering comes the pleasurable task of harvesting your allotment crops, either to eat immediately or to store for later. With good planning and organization you can enjoy allotment produce almost every day of the year.

YOUR ALLOTMENT PRODUCE

The tips and suggestions here are just a few of the good ideas for harvesting and enjoying your allotment produce. You will always get the best flavour and quality if you preserve fruit and vegetables when they are really fresh. Plastic supermarket cartons are good for harvesting. Keep a stock of foil trays and hole-free plastic bags for freezing. If you like jam and chutney, remember to save jars through the year so you have plenty to hand. For chutney and pickles you need lids with corrosion-resistant lid linings. As a rule, all vegetables and fruit freeze best if they have a lower water content. Almost any vegetable will make a soup.

VEGETABLES

When harvesting allotment vegetables, do some of the preparation and trimming at the allotment. Put all but the woodiest material on the compost heap and remove or destroy any diseased tissue. Apart from the specific preparations included below, be sure to trim and wash all vegetables extremely well before you use them. And beware of clinging wildlife. The worst can be washed off at the plot if you have water handy.

For freezing, most books recommend blanching vegetables – plunging them quickly into boiling water then cooling them speedily – before freezing, but this is not always necessary, especially if you're going to use the produce fairly quickly. Experiment and see what works best for you. To stop peas, beans and soft fruit from sticking together, open freeze them on trays, if you have the space, before bagging and labelling them.

BEANS AND PEAS

Among the most enjoyable crops to grow and eat, beans and peas are ideal candidates for freezing and preserving.

Broad beans

Always best harvested when young – they quickly get big and floury. Test a few pods for bean size before you pick them. They

For an eco-friendly alternative to avocado, use cooked and skinned broad beans to make a dip by processing them with olive oil, garlic and a generous squeeze of lime juice. Season them well with salt and freshly ground black pepper. Add a little chilli sauce for an extra kick.

freeze excellently. Before serving them, especially when larger, pop them out of their tougher outer skins. The shoot tips, removed to discourage blackfly, are also edible as long as you pick them when unaffected and are a real delicacy.
If pods do 'go over', let them mature and keep the beans to plant next year. Take the empty pods back to the plot for compost.

French beans

These need frequent picking to ensure you get them at their best. Dwarf French beans are very shallow rooted and it is easy to uproot plants accidentally as you pick. Using scissors to snip beans off is a good move, or hold the plant with one hand while you nip off the stalk at the end of each bean with finger and thumb. French beans, especially round ones picked small, freeze well whole, and are good for stir fries.

In the Kitchen

Lightly cooked French beans are ideal for salads – try them whole with tomatoes and basil – and essential for a *niçoise*. The purple ones turn a lovely dark green when cooked.

Borlotti and haricot beans

These need to be left on the plants until the pods are crisp and dry, which will probably be September or October. Pick them on a dry day and put them in the sun or a warm place until the pods are crisp, then shell them and spread the beans out on trays to dry completely. Store in airtight jars. Use them through the year for everything from soups and stews to chilli.

Runner beans

Runner beans need picking regularly, before they get stringy and 'beany'. If you miss some, take them off when you spot them and throw them into the compost or leave them and keep the seeds for next year. Larger ones will need their sides 'stringing' before they are sliced and cooked. They freeze well, even without blanching, and are successful in stir fries and curries. The old fashioned method of putting them through a mechanical slicer is quick and efficient but can mar their structure and flavour.

Use excess runner beans to make a chutney. It will keep for 9 months. 'String' larger beans before slicing them.

Runner bean chutney

2 kg runner beans, sliced medium thinly

750 g onions, peeled and chopped

4 heaped tbs cornflour

1½ tbs turmeric

1 tsp each salt, dry mustard, ginger and cayenne pepper

850 ml malt vinegar

1 kg Demerara sugar

1 Cook and drain the beans well.
2 Cook the onions in 500 ml vinegar for 10 minutes, add the beans and cook for another 5 minutes. Allow to cool a little.
3 Mix the dry ingredients with about 250 ml of the vinegar to make a very smooth paste. Add gradually to the bean and onion mixture, stirring well to avoid lumps and bring back to the boil.
4 Add the sugar and cook for about 20 minutes until thick.
5 Cool, bottle and label.

Peas

Of all allotment vegetables, peas freeze perfectly if you are lucky enough to have any surplus. Pick peas when the pods feel firm and full – but not hard and floury – which may be daily. Test them by popping a few. Any that do go over can be left, then be harvested and dried like haricots. Watch out for any grubs in the pods and don't forget to compost them. Sugar snaps can also be frozen but are just as good sliced and added to a salad.

Unlike 'regular' peas, mange touts do not freeze well, which is why it is best to plant them in succession so you are not overloaded, although they will keep in the fridge for up to a week. Cook and serve mange touts as you would ordinary peas. Raw or lightly cooked and cooled, and with sun dried tomatoes, feta cheese and mint they make a great salad.

In the Kitchen

Peas are ideal for soup (traditionally with ham) and like broad beans can make an excellent dip. Mint is their perfect herb pairing. Add them to a risotto or braise them gently French style with quarters of hearted lettuce, spring onions and vegetable stock.

BRASSICAS

When you harvest brassicas, compost the leaves unless diseased, but because the stems can take years to rot, either chop them up for compost or take them to your local recycling centre. Endlessly versatile, they can be enjoyed all year.

Cabbage

Most modern cabbages stand reasonably well, but you need to pick and eat them before the heads 'blow' (and even flower) or before they get mushy on the outside and riddled with snails and slugs. Any good cabbage will have a firm head, and even one that's past its best can probably be used if you cut off and compost all the outside leaves. If you don't need to clear the ground immediately, try cutting off the heads with a sharp knife and leaving the stumps in place. Small clumps of leaves should sprout from these, which can be picked and eaten.

Crisp white or pale cabbage, and tender red cabbage, are great eaten cooked or raw, but the darker green varieties are better cooked. Red cabbage freezes very well if you casserole it with onions, garlic and red wine, plus strips of orange rind for extra flavour.

Fermented foods are now widely promoted as health enhancers. For sauerkraut use crisp cabbage with solid hearts and make sure all your equipment and jars are sterilized before you begin, and your hands clean.

Sauerkraut

1 kg cabbage thinly shredded
15 g sea salt
2 or 3 bay leaves
½ tsp caraway seeds

1 Put the cabbage and salt into a large bowl. Mix for 10 minutes with your hands, squeezing out as much liquid as possible.
2 Pack into one or two mason jars or large preserving jars, pressing it down hard with a pestle or similar implement then pour the liquid on top. Add the bay leaves and caraway seeds.
3 Make sure the cabbage is totally covered, if not make a brine with 25 g of salt in 100 ml of water to top it up.
4 Leave in a cool place at around 18°C for 3-10 days, pressing the cabbage down each day and topping up the liquid as necessary until it stops bubbling. Remove any scum that forms.
5 Once you are happy with the flavour, refrigerate for up to 6 months.

Kale

To enjoy kale at its most tender, take out the central heart first, as this will encourage the growth of new side shoots. It can be used like any dark green cabbage, but is best if well chopped. Very finely shredded deep fried kale is the 'seaweed' served topped with brown sugar in Chinese restaurants, and easy to make at home.

Brussels sprouts

It is said that frost improves the flavour of sprouts, which is fine if they are a frost resistant variety, but will otherwise make them mushy. Pick sprouts from the bottom of the stem, taking them from a few plants each time. Before and as you pick, remove any yellowing leaves. At the end of the season cut off and eat the head – a bonus when there are few fresh vegetables. Cooked sprouts, the obligatory accompaniment to the Christmas turkey are not everyone's favourite, but sprout lovers relish

In the Kitchen

A salad surprise. To raw, finely sliced sprouts add about half the quantity of grated carrot and some chopped walnuts. Mix in a dressing made with a mixture of equal quantities of mayonnaise and low fat crème fraîche seasoned with salt and pepper and a dash of orange juice.

them with bacon and garlic, with roast chestnuts, or in a soup flavoured with nutmeg. Small, tight, blanched sprouts will freeze well.

Calabrese

If you cut the heads of calabrese and leave plants intact, side shoots and extra small heads will, with luck, be produced around the top of the stem. Heads are best sliced off with a knife. Calabrese is versatile, though best parboiled before being added to stir fries or used in a salad. Try it in vegetable curry or cooked au gratin exactly as for cauliflower.

Sprouting broccoli

Said to be the poor man's asparagus, sprouting broccoli needs picking little and often – with your fingers or with the help of a knife – and the more you pick the more you get. It is delicious steamed or boiled and served hot with butter, warm with a French dressing, or cold. It is best eaten fresh as it doesn't freeze well.

Chinese broccoli

The top few inches of the flowering stalks of Chinese broccoli should be picked as soon as the flowers appear, which can be as little as a couple of months after sowing. Cook it lightly then serve it in a hoisin or black bean sauce with some spring onions or garlic. A sprinkling of cashew nuts or some chopped pickled ginger added makes it extra tasty.

Cauliflower

As your cauliflowers mature, begin harvesting them when they are quite small. If you don't you will have a glut, though they will keep for a week or two if hung upside down in a cool place and sprayed daily with cold water. Use a sharp knife to cut off each head, including a good number of protective leaves.

Use cauliflower as you would calabrese; for salads it can be eaten raw or almost cooked before being dressed while still warm. It also roasts well.

Chinese cabbage

These are excellent for stir fries, kimchi (see radishes) and salads. Cutting the heads of mature plants will encourage new leaves to grow from the stump of a well-established root. If plants do flower, cut the stalks and use them like broccoli.

Pak choi and Mizuna

When very small these can be picked and eaten raw. When larger they are ideal for stir fries served over rice or noodles. Try boiling or steaming pak choi very lightly then adding some quickly fried garlic and/or spring onions and soy sauce. Peanuts and fish sauce are other tasty additions. Small hearty pak choi can be parboiled then braised in the oven.

"Begin harvesting cauliflowers when they are quite small...."

Quick cauliflower curry

1 head of cauliflower broken up and parboiled or lightly steamed
1 or 2 garlic cloves, chopped
1 medium onion, chopped
1 red chilli, chopped
1 tsp mustard seeds
1 tbs garam masala
2 -3 tbs sesame oil
400 ml coconut milk
Salt and freshly ground black pepper

1 Fry the garlic, onions, chilli for about 5 minutes until soft. Stir in the spices.
2 Add the cauliflower and coconut milk and cook until the cauliflower is tender. Season to taste with salt and pepper.

LEAFY VEGETABLES

Harvesting little and often is the key to success with leafy vegetables which are always best when enjoyed young and tender. Because of their high water content they can be successfully juiced.

Spinach

Leaves of spinach need picking little and often if possible. One good way of preventing it going to seed too quickly is to pick any central shoots that look as if they are about to bolt. Although fresh leaves are full of water, cooked spinach freezes well. Small, tender spinach leaves are excellent in salads. When cooking spinach there is no need to add any water if you start it on a very low heat with a drizzle of oil. A grating of nutmeg gives an excellent flavour. A mixture of spinach and butter puréed in a blender makes a quick sauce for pasta or meat balls. Spinach can be added direct to a stir fry or curry. Blanched and well dried spinach can be added to pasta dough for a vibrant green colour, or added to a quiche or tart. A spinach salad, alone or with other leaves is perfect simply dressed with a mixture of olive oil, mustard and lemon juice.

Swiss chard

Like spinach, chard is best picked young, before it has a chance for the leaves to get bitter and the stems stringy. The leaves can be used like spinach but pack a stronger flavour. The stems, which are often tastier than the leaves, can be cooked and served whole, either plain or with a sauce, or chopped and added to any vegetable dish.

Spinach soup

25 g butter
2 tbs rapeseed oil
1 bunch spring onions, roughly chopped
150 g new (baby) potatoes, washed and chopped
750 ml vegetable stock
450 g spinach, washed
Freshly grated nutmeg, to taste
100 ml single cream
Salt and freshly ground pepper

1 Melt the butter with the oil. Add the onions and potato and fry for about 5 minutes until the onion is soft and the potato lightly browned.
2 Add the stock and simmer for 15 to 20 minutes until the potato is cooked.
3 Add the spinach and nutmeg and cook for about 10 minutes until the spinach has collapsed and is tender.
4 Cool a little, then check the seasoning.
5 Process in a blender, adding half the cream.
6 Reheat to just below boiling, then serve with the remaining cream swirled into each bowl.

EDIBLE STEMS

The delicacy of edible stems means that they need to be harvested and used with care, but are some of the highlights of the allotment harvest.

Asparagus

To harvest allotment asparagus, you need a sharp knife for cutting off spears just below ground level. This helps reduce the aroma so attractive to asparagus beetles. By tradition, you should stop harvesting asparagus on the longest day – June 21st – but you should always stop cutting it after six to eight weeks. Cut spears regularly and don't worry if you miss some. Just let them grow naturally into their 'ferns' which, after the harvest is over, need to be left to grow for the rest of the summer. If you have a few spears and need more to make a meal, put them in iced water for a few hours, then wrap them in kitchen paper, put them into a plastic bag and refrigerate them until you need them. Served simply with butter, hollandaise or vinaigrette asparagus is unfailingly delicious.

Celery

To prevent damage to the stalks, celery is best lifted with a fork. You will need to harvest self-blanching varieties before they get damaged by frost. Keep the green tops to use as herbs or add them to the stock pot or stir fry. If you have more celery than you can use, freeze it after cooking (for instance braised or made into soup).

In the Kitchen

For quick snacks, fill celery stalks with softened cream cheese or smoked salmon or smoked mackerel pâté, then cut them into bite-sized lengths. Celery braised in vegetable stock and cooked in a lidded pan on the stove top with some onions and herbs added makes an excellent dish.

In the Kitchen

There is no need to cut an asparagus spear before you cook it. Bend it gently and it will snap at the point where the woodier base begins. The ends are great for asparagus or any vegetable stock or soup. Asparagus can be steamed, grilled or boiled or added to a quiche or open tart. Large spears are best cooked upright in a pan part filled with water so that the tips steam and the bases boil.

To make a fennel salad, chop it finely and add to finely sliced raw courgettes and some cooked and cooled broad beans. Add a little lemon juice and a mustardy French dressing. Let the mixture marinade for about 30 minutes before serving.

Florence fennel

Fennel can be used much as celery, but is an even better match with fish. Trim the roots off plants as you lift them and cut back the tops; in late season keep some to use when the herb fennel is over. Stir fried with onions and potatoes it makes a perfect accompaniment to any seafood.

Kohlrabi

Best pulled and eaten when small and tender, and their tastiest when raw (they may need peeling), kohlrabi have a mild turnip like flavour. They are also excellent roasted or stir fried with the leafy tops included in any Asian recipe.

ROOT VEGETABLES

From potatoes and carrots to parsnips and swedes, root vegetable are kitchen staples high in nutrients and extraordinarily versatile.

Radishes

Pull your radishes regularly – initially to thin a row – and eat them young. Big winter radishes can be left in the ground until you need them or harvested and stored in a box in a cool dark place. They are best grated or very finely sliced and perfect simply dipped in salt as a snack.

Use mooli or regular radishes to make kimchi with Chinese cabbage. Experiment with different proportions of the ingredients.

Basic kimchi

1 head Chinese cabbage, thinly sliced
3 garlic cloves, crushed
1 tbs sea salt
2 tbs grated fresh ginger
2 tbs chilli sauce
1 tbs light brown sugar
3 tbs cider vinegar
About 12 regular radishes or 1 good sized mooli, grated
1 small onion, finely chopped

1 Mix the cabbage and salt and leave for 1 hour.
2 Mix the garlic, ginger, chilli sauce, sugar and vinegar.
3 Rinse the cabbage well, spin in a salad spinner then dry on kitchen paper or a tea towel so that it is as dry as possible.
4 Thoroughly mix all the ingredients together then put into jars, seal and leave to ferment overnight. Refrigerate and eat within 2 weeks.

Beetroot

The beetroot crop begins with adding the leaves of thinnings to salads – they mix brilliantly with bacon and avocado. Roots can then be lifted and used as you need them. If you have some left in the ground in autumn, either pull them up and use them for pickles, or secure some fleece over them as frost protection. Alternatively, pull them and store them in a box of peat in a cool dark place.

To prevent beetroot from bleeding, and to help preserve their flavour, wash them well, then boil, bake or microwave them in their skins. (If microwaving, wrap them individually in cling film and turn them several times during cooking.) Alternatively peel and chop large beetroot into 2 cm (¾ in) cubes, put them in a bowl with a few tablespoons of water, cover and microwave on high for 5 minutes. Stir and repeat once or twice until tender, then drain.

In the Kitchen

More ways with beetroot:
- Peel and chop then bake them in foil with oil and chopped red onions.
- When using beetroot for a borsch to serve hot or cold, add lemon juice or a can of tomatoes to prevent it being too sweet. Flavour with fresh rosemary.
- Boil tiny, tender beetroot and serve with a mustard and mayonnaise dressing.
- Make a beetroot 'coleslaw', by tossing raw, grated beetroot in a mixture of French dressing, mayonnaise, yoghurt and horseradish sauce.

"Beetroot can be lifted and used as you need them...."

Carrots

When harvesting carrots, use a fork to make them easier to lift, then trim the tops and keep them to use as a fresh herb or in a salad. The crop can be left in the ground over winter, but is best covered with fleece for frost protection. If you have a cool dark space suitable for storage (but always protected from rodents) lift and trim them, check for soundness and pack them in boxes of dry sand. Be selective; black indentations and tunnels made by carrot fly attack can be hard to spot until you actually scrape or peel them. If you have a freezer big enough, they can be blanched and frozen. They are good juiced or added to kimchi.

Celeriac

Unless you can be sure of keeping it from frost damage, celeriac needs to be eaten before the ground gets icy, or lifted in November and stored in sand, as for carrots. It also freezes well if pre-cooked. However the roots will carry on swelling right through the autumn. Because the flesh quickly discolours on contact with air, celeriac benefits from being put into water with lemon juice added as you peel and chop it. It is excellent grated and eaten raw, roasted or boiled and mashed, either on its own or with potato. Fish and bacon are both excellent partners. A celeriac soup is also delicious, and can have tart apple added to extend the flavour range.

In the Kitchen

Versatile carrots, both raw and cooked:
- Make a carrot and coriander soup.
- Bake a carrot cake.
- Grate and add to cabbage, chives and pumpkin seeds for a crunchy coleslaw.
- Brush with honey or a flavoured oil and roast. (Excellent in the air fryer.)
- Roast and blitz with sour cream, garlic granules and ginger for a dip.
- Add lightly cooked warm carrots to a salad with olives, lemon juice, honey and coriander.

Celeriac steaks

Peel the celeriac and cut 2 cm (¾ in) steaks from the centre, then brush generously with olive oil mixed with some Dijon mustard. Roast in a 180°C oven for 40 minutes, turning them halfway through. Serve with a salsa verde made from tarragon, parsley, capers, garlic, white wine vinegar and a little more mustard, well seasoned with sea salt and freshly ground black pepper.

Parsnips

As soon as their foliage begins to fade, parsnips are ready to lift with a fork. They are usually frost hardy so can be left in the ground all winter. In spring, any parsnips you haven't eaten will start to sprout green tops again. By this stage they are usually very woody so the cores will need cutting out. Destroy any badly affected by canker. They freeze well. Parsnips are excellent roasted (brush them with honey for extra sweetness), boiled and mashed, and are good in casseroles. Curried parsnip soup is highly recommended, or add them to a curry with chickpeas for a meat free meal.

Turnips

To prevent them getting woody and over pungent, turnips need pulling regularly when small or lifting with a fork – ideally they should get no larger than tennis balls. Winter turnips can be left until you need them, while summer ones can be peeled, blanched and frozen. Don't forget that the green tops are edible either fresh or cooked.

In the Kitchen

Add peeled, chopped raw baby turnips to a salad with tart apples and spring onions or grate and add them to a slaw.

Swedes

Totally frost tolerant, swedes are the archetypal winter vegetable. Use a fork to lift them as you need them. You can pull them in October when they are still quite small, and store them in a cool place in your shed or garage (as long as they are safe from rodents). Swedes can be tough to peel and cut. Boiled and mashed with plenty of butter and pepper they are the 'neeps' that make a traditional accompaniment to haggis. For extra flavour try adding some ground ginger.

"Parsnips freeze well and are excellent roasted...."

Potatoes

Even if you are not growing earlies you may want to harvest some main crop as 'new' potatoes. If so, they should be lifted when they are about the size of hens' eggs. You can test whether they're ready by using your hands to push the soil away from a plant at the end of a row. For a main crop, test the skin before you lift them. If it scrapes off easily when rubbed with your thumb, then it is ready.

When digging or lifting potatoes you need to be careful not to spike them. Try to insert the fork at least 15 cm (6 in) away from the stem. As you pick the potatoes out of the ground (a companion is invaluable) check that any potatoes you want to keep long term are undamaged by the fork or by wireworms. Discard any that are green, which can be poisonous if eaten. If the soil and crop are wet, leave them on the soil surface for a day or two to dry out. Go back along the row to make sure you have removed as many as possible, though it is virtually impossible to collect all the tiny ones that spring up as 'volunteers' the following year.

Traditionally, sound potatoes are stored in 'breathable' hessian sacks and kept in a dark, cool place. For many this is impossible, and a sack kept in the shed is likely to be quickly eaten by hungry rodents. However they will store reasonably well in a metal dustbin between layers of newspaper.

There are endless ways to enjoy potatoes, whether baked, boiled, roasted or fried. And there is nothing better than the first new potatoes of the year slathered in butter or olive oil. Old fashioned potato cakes made with maincrop produce are delicious. Add extra butter to serve. They are especially good a part of a traditional breakfast.

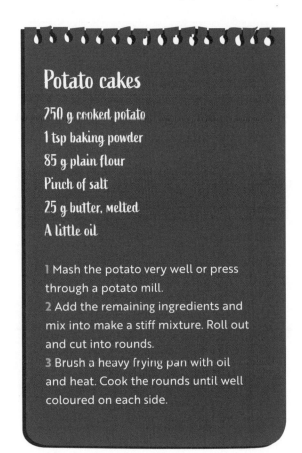

Potato cakes

750 g cooked potato
1 tsp baking powder
85 g plain flour
Pinch of salt
25 g butter, melted
A little oil

1 Mash the potato very well or press through a potato mill.
2 Add the remaining ingredients and mix into make a stiff mixture. Roll out and cut into rounds.
3 Brush a heavy frying pan with oil and heat. Cook the rounds until well coloured on each side.

Sweet potatoes

As versatile as the regular potatoes but don't keep well so need to be eaten before the end of the season. Cooked, they will freeze well if you have the space.

Jerusalem artichokes

These hardy tubers will survive right through the winter in the ground. As with potatoes, it is worth the effort to pick out all the minute tubers, which will readily sprout again. As a vegetable, artichokes can be used in all the same ways as other root vegetables. They pair particularly well with hazelnuts and sage. Artichoke soup is an all-time favourite.

THE ONION FAMILY

No good cook will ever be without onions of all kinds – and garlic – the essential flavourings for innumerable dishes. For eating uncooked, spring and red onions have the mildest flavour. Shallots are also mild and perfect for pickling.

Onions

When onions are nearly ready to harvest the leaves begin to turn yellow, at which point bend over the tops and leave them for a couple of weeks. Then, ideally in a dry, sunny spell, dig or gently pull them up and leave them upside down to ripen off for about a week. Don't be tempted to cut off the tops before they have died back properly or you may encourage the entry of rot. If the weather is wet you may need to put them in your shed or even take them home to a garage or a spare room to dry completely. Mesh trays are ideal for drying both onions and garlic. Once ripe they can be hung in a string or put in string bags and hung in a cool, dry place away from direct sunlight. Keep a regular check on them and remove and destroy any that look as if they are beginning to rot.

An onion marmalade is a perfect accompaniment to many dishes. It will keep in the fridge for up to 6 months.

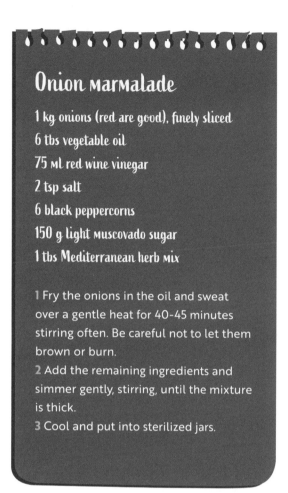

Onion marmalade

1 kg onions (red are good), finely sliced
6 tbs vegetable oil
75 ml red wine vinegar
2 tsp salt
6 black peppercorns
150 g light muscovado sugar
1 tbs Mediterranean herb mix

1 Fry the onions in the oil and sweat over a gentle heat for 40-45 minutes stirring often. Be careful not to let them brown or burn.
2 Add the remaining ingredients and simmer gently, stirring, until the mixture is thick.
3 Cool and put into sterilized jars.

Spring onions

Pull or lift spring onions with a fork as you need them – but remember that if growing close together they can break off if you pull them with your hands. Midsummer plantings will last right through until spring. Any that go to flower can be used like garden alliums for decoration.

Shallots

After pulling shallots need to be separated out, left for a few days to ripen in the sun, then hung up in a net in a cool place for the winter. To make them easier to peel and prepare a good trick is to immerse them in boiling water for a few minutes. They pack a real punch as pickled onions or an ingredient of piccalilli.

Garlic

Unless you are growing the variety 'Mediterranean', which makes flower stems as part of its normal growth (and needs cutting back 2 or 3 weeks before lifting), garlic is best harvested before it flowers. You will certainly want to use some fresh or 'wet' garlic for its superbly mild flavour – whole heads are delicious when roasted. For storage, lift bulbs gently with a fork, ideally in a spell of dry weather, and leave them in the open to ripen. When dry they can be strung up and kept in a waterproof shed or in a cool, dry spot at home.

For a subtle hint of garlic use it as a rub on meat or vegetables, or the inside of a salad bowl.

In the Kitchen

When cooking with garlic, be careful not to burn it or it will taste bitter. It is often better added later in a recipe to prevent this. Some extra ways to get the most from your crop:
• Put peeled cloves into bottles of olive or other vegetable oil and leave for a few weeks.
• Pickle cloves in a mixture of white wine and balsamic vinegar with spices such as coriander seeds and dried chilli.
• Make aioli, the classic garlic mayonnaise.
• Add crushed cloves raw or lightly cooked to mashed potato alone or with herbs.
• Make a chermoula by crushing cloves with cumin and coriander seeds then adding lemon juice, vinegar and cayenne pepper to taste.
• Add cloves unpeeled when you roast meat or vegetables. Be careful when you squeeze out the soft insides – they can squirt and are boiling hot.

Leeks

You can begin lifting leeks (use a fork) when they are small and tender. The tops and roots can be trimmed off at the plot and composted. They will continue growing slowly right through until late spring, although may well have woody centres by then. If you want to clear the ground, any excess will freeze well, cooked, and are useful in summer for making vichyssoise. Always be sure to wash leeks extra thoroughly. If you want to use them whole, make two cuts, at right angles, down the centre of each and wash them under running water.

In the Kitchen

Leeks can often give dishes a milder flavour than onions. Some good ways to try them are:
· Cook baby leeks whole and serve warm in a vinaigrette.
· Add to a risotto.
· Cook and add to potato and kale or cabbage to make a colcannon.
· Use for a soup. Try a classic cock-a-leekie or cook them with barley and top with crispy bacon bites. Or mix with spinach and peas.
· With chicken leeks make a perfect pie filling, topped with pastry or mashed potato. Or add to cheese for a meat free option.

"Always be sure to wash leeks extra thoroughly...."

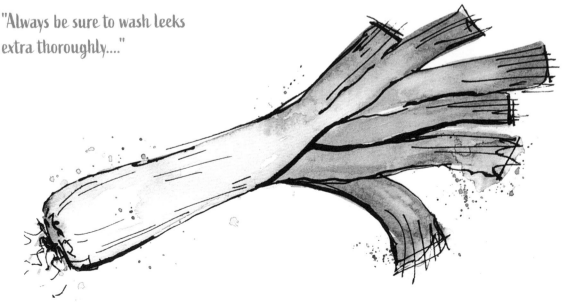

VEGETABLE FRUITS

Harvesting the first vegetable fruits of the season is a sure sign that summer has arrived. At the end of the season, many will keep as reminders of warm days, whether dried like winter squashes or as a tomato sauce or chutney.

Courgettes

Of all allotment excesses, courgettes take the prize. And small ones can explode into 'marrows' overnight. Pick them regularly – ideally by hand to prevent the spread of viruses – when they are about 12 cm (5 in) long. Large ones will keep several weeks in a cool dark place.

Because of their high water content, the best way to freeze them is in tomato sauce or as a ratatouille, or puréed as a basis for soups. Overlarge fruit may need its central core of seeds removed to make it palatable.

Marrows

Marrows need cutting with a knife as you harvest them. If you have spare marrows at the end of the season, they will keep well in a cool dark place like a garage, ideally strung in individual nets. They are excellent halved lengthwise, scooped out and stuffed, or the flesh can be cubed and baked. Spaghetti marrows are

In the Kitchen

Some more ways with courgettes:
• Sliced crosswise and sautéed in olive oil with basil or tarragon (and garlic), or with lemon juice and pesto.
• In a courgette, tomato and onion frittata.
• Stuffed courgette (scooped out, microwaved for 5 minutes, stuffed and oven baked for 45 minutes). Good stuffings are rice or breadcrumbs with cheese or cooked meat added and onion for flavouring.
• Courgette soup – with onions or leeks, lemon and herbs such as tarragon, topped with yoghurt (also excellent cold).
• Courgette and potato gratin.
• Courgette ribbon salad. Try adding anchovies, capers, preserved lemons or chopped gherkins.
• Courgette couscous – with herbs and, if you like, garlic and/or onions, tomatoes
• Courgette niçoise – substitute cooked or raw courgettes for green beans in this classic salad.
• Courgettes chopped and fried with prawns and lemon served with tagliatelle pasta.
• Courgette flowers stuffed with ricotta and fried.
• A courgette cake, although not to everyone's taste.

best baked whole and the cooked flesh spooned out and used like pasta. Marrow and ginger jam is also delicious.

Squashes and Pumpkins

These are ready to harvest if, when tapped, they produce a slightly hollow sound. They can be cut early when small but are less likely to keep. Thanks to their thick skins, both will keep all winter in a cool dark place. Just peel, cut into chunks and use. For pumpkin pie the flesh needs to be puréed, sieved and cooled before use. And of course they are essential for carving at Halloween.

In the Kitchen

Both quashes and pumpkins are excellent curried and will make soups of many kinds which can be topped with cooked chestnuts at Christmas. Steamed pumpkin mixed with half its raw weight of dark Muscovado sugar, the juice of 2 lemons and some mace, nutmeg and cinnamon to taste, then simmered for a good hour or more until thick, makes a spiced pumpkin butter delicious on toast.

"Both squashes and pumpkins are excellent curried and will make soups of many kinds...."

Tomatoes

Allotment tomatoes have the best flavour when picked fully ripe, but if, as autumn approaches, you still have lots of green fruit, don't discard them. Green tomatoes are excellent stir fried, or as a classic chutney ingredient. They may also ripen in a basket in an airing cupboard – adding a ripe banana can help. Larger fruit can also be individually wrapped in tissue paper and put in a drawer or a cardboard box. It is always handy to have a stock of tomato sauce or purée in the freezer and worth the trouble of peeling them first. Pouring boiling water over them will split the skins to make the job easier.

Tomato chutney is a classic. This recipe also works with ripe fruit.

Easy green tomato chutney

1 kg green tomatoes, chopped

400 g onions, finely chopped

1 medium cooking apple, peeled and chopped

400 ml pickling vinegar

100 g sultanas

2 tsp mustard seeds

2 tsp ground ginger

2 tsp salt

150 g light Muscovado sugar

1 Put the tomatoes, onions, apple and 200 ml vinegar into a large, heavy saucepan. Heat until boiling then cook gently for 30-45 minutes, stirring frequently, until tender.
2 Stir in the remaining ingredients and cook for another 30 minutes or until thick.
3 Cool, spoon into sterilized jars, label and seal.

Cucumbers

Outdoor cucumbers are best picked when small, before they have a chance to get bitter, but do need peeling before they are eaten. The seeds will also need to be scooped out of large ones. Excesses will freeze well as a soup (to serve cold) made by puréeing cucumbers with light stock, spring onions, mint and yoghurt. They are also good in chutneys and pickles. Pair them with dill for an unmistakeable mid-European flavour.

Gherkins

Pick gherkins regularly as they mature and use them for pickles. Add heads of dill flowers for an authentic flavour. For each 500 g of produce you will need 500 ml vinegar and 100 g of salt. Other good flavourings are allspice, juniper berries, bay leaves and fennel and mustard seeds.

Cucamelons

Slice cucamelons into salads or salsas or pickle them like gherkins. They also work well in stir fries. Or add them to a gin and tonic or jug of Pimm's for an interesting twist.

Chilled cucumber soup

1 large or 3 or 4 small cucumbers, peeled, deseeded and chopped

500 – 750 ml well flavoured vegetable stock

4 spring onions, chopped (raw or very lightly fried until soft)

4 - 6 tablespoons plain yoghurt

Leaves from 1 or 2 sprigs of mint

Salt and pepper

Croutons and chopped chives, to serve

1 Blend all the ingredients thoroughly using 500 ml of the stock. Dilute as necessary with the remainder.

2 Adjust the seasoning, remembering that it needs to be very well seasoned. If it is too thick add the rest of the stock (or more yoghurt) and adjust the seasoning, then cool in the fridge.

3 Serve sprinkled with the croutons and chives.

Sweetcorn

To test sweetcorn for ripeness, pull apart the leafy sheath around a cob and press a nail into one of the seeds, which should be plump and pale yellow. If it exudes a creamy liquid, then it is ready to pick and eat or freeze. They freeze excellently, either on or off their cobs. To remove corn kernels, hold the cob upright then use a sharp knife to cut downwards, near the core of each cob. Don't forget to compost all the outer leaves and threads.

In the Kitchen

A fresh cob, boiled or grilled and served with butter, salt and pepper is one of the delights of late summer. Try some of these other ways with allotment produce:
• Make fritters adding kernels to a basic batter.
• Add with bacon to a classic chowder or make a chicken and sweetcorn soup.
• Mix a salsa using sweetcorn, spring onions and chopped green chilli and red pepper.
• Create a salad with celery, olives and feta cheese.

Globe artichokes

When they are full but firm, cut off large globes with a knife or secateurs, beginning with the topmost or 'king' head. As you do so, take the opportunity to strengthen the plant by cutting back each stem to about half its original length. If you miss some and they flower, cut off the whole stems and use for stunning flower arrangements.

Before you cook globe artichokes, trim the stems level with the base. If you wish you can snip the tips off the leafy flower scales, too. Then boil them in water with some lemon juice added to prevent discolouration. Test for doneness by pulling away one of the outermost scales – it should come away easily. Otherwise, pull apart the topmost ones and pull out both the small inner scales, followed by the hairy choke, for which you will need the help of a spoon. Serve them with a vinaigrette. Cooked chokes can be successfully preserved in olive oil. Add garlic and/or herbs for extra flavour.

SALAD LEAVES

The way you harvest your salads depends on what you're growing, but many can be picked as handfuls or bags of leaves until the plants are spent or go to seed. All are best eaten as fresh as possible, but will keep for several days in the fridge. All need washing well.

Lettuce

Pick the leaves of cut and come again lettuce as you need them. As you harvest whole heads trim them at the plot and put roots and rough outer leaves into the compost. Small, hearty lettuces like 'Little Gem' can be cut in half lengthwise, brushed with oil and grilled or tossed in the frying pan.

In the Kitchen

Lettuce inspirations.
• Use leaves as 'containers' for all kinds of snacks. Fill with anything from prawns in a lemon mayonnaise or mixes of baby vegetables such as carrots, cabbage and turnips chopped and dressed.
• Make into wraps for Asian style mixtures of all kinds.
• Ring the changes with dressings by adding allotment grown fresh herbs.
• Make into a juice for green goodness.

Rocket

For small quantities, pick rocket leaf by leaf. For more, cut whole stalks and strip the leaves carefully by hand from bottom to top. In salads rocket is best mixed with less stringent ingredients such as lettuce, cucumber, celery and avocado.

In the Kitchen

ROCKET PESTO

A deeply flavoured change from the basil version. Blend 100 g rocket leaves with 50 g pine nuts, 50 g parmesan or pecorino cheese (or vegan alternative), 150 ml olive oil and ½ tsp powdered garlic with salt and pepper to taste. It will keep in the fridge for up to 5 days.

Radicchio and Chicory

Radicchio is a good winter stand by and can last through until April in mild winters if covered with fleece or a cloche before the first frosts arrive. Grilled figs topped with goat's cheese make perfect partners for radicchio. Cut the heads of forcing chicory and use them like lettuce, both raw and cooked. Larger individual leaves can be brushed with oil and charred quickly on a very hot grill pan or heavy based saucepan.

Corn salad and Land cress

It is fiddly to pick off individual leaves of these crops so you may prefer to harvest plants whole and just trim off the roots once a good rosette of leaves has formed. Because they grow close to the ground the leaves will need particularly careful washing.

HERBS

All allotment herbs are ideal for using fresh as you need them and are the essentials of well flavoured sauces, broths and soups of all kinds. Those with soft leaves will keep their flavour chopped and frozen in ice cube trays. Unless you are growing them for seed, harvest the herbs that you plan to freeze or dry just before they flower, when their flavour will be most intense. Ideal for this treatment are parsley, dill, fennel, tarragon, chervil, mint and lovage. Bay leaves packed in plastic pots also freeze well.

Many herbs can also be cut, hung in a warm dry place, dried and stored in airtight jars. Good for this treatment are sage, tarragon, thyme, rosemary and marjoram (oregano). These can also make good additions to potpourris. Another great use for them is as flavoured oils to add to dressings or used as a finish for all kinds of savoury dishes. Chives are a favourite. Herbs infused with boiling water make soothing drinks and herbal preparations are widely used medicinally, but always consult a reliable reference before making and using them in this way at home.

In the Kitchen

- Any fresh herbs mashed into butter or added as whole sprigs to olive oil make versatile ingredients. Herb butters freeze remarkably well, too. If you want to add garlic this is best done after defrosting.
- For flavouring curries and other spicy dishes, allow some plants to go to seed. Pick and dry the heads, then shake out the seeds into a bag before storing them in airtight jars. Best are coriander, fennel and dill.
- Many herbs including mint, rosemary and sage make excellent jellies.
- For sweet dishes, add herbs to sugar in a jar in alternate layers and leave to infuse for a week before using.

Rosemary

Unequal as a partner for lamb and key to a bouquet garni. Also brilliant for flavouring bread, whether made with yeast or a flatbread. Use branches from which the leaves have been stripped as kebab sticks for additional flavour.

Sage

Marry sage with pork in all its forms. Fried sage leaves are hugely versatile. Add them to soups, pasta, risottos and salads.

Bay

Pairs well with fish, whether cooked in a parcel or in a sauce. Always remember to remove bay leaves before serving a dish as they can be unpleasant if swallowed.

Thyme

Cut individual sprigs and add them to a bouquet garni or strip the leaves by hand. Thyme is best used in a similar way to rosemary, but leave plenty to flower and attract bees and other pollinators.

Tarragon

Has a mild aniseed flavour that pairs well with lemon. It will enliven any chicken dish. Add tarragon to a bottle of white wine vinegar and infuse for a week before straining and using.

Mint

A most versatile herb way beyond mint sauces and jellies and a flavouring for new potatoes. Add it to salads and add chopped leaves to servings of courgettes, tomatoes and other vegetables. A tea made with fresh mint is a delight.

In the Kitchen

QUICK MINT SAUCE

Wash and dry a generous handful of mint leaves. Chop finely then sprinkle with 2 tsp of caster sugar. Put into a bowl and pour over 2 tbs of boiling water. Add 2 tbs of white wine vinegar and leave to steep for 30 minutes before using.

Marjoram and Oregano

Both these herbs are at their best when dried to enhance their flavour. They are excellent paired with tomatoes and potatoes and in any Mediterranean recipe.

Lemon balm and Lemon verbena

The citrus flavour of these herbs makes them ideal companions for fish, but they also work in sweet dishes such as stone fruit poached in syrup.

Lovage

Best use as a mild form of celery, lovage makes an excellent soup that also freezes well.

Lovage soup

1 tbs vegetable oil

25 g butter

1 bunch of spring onions, chopped

250 g new potatoes, washed and chopped

500 ml vegetable or chicken stock

30 g lovage leaves, chopped

Salt and freshly ground black pepper

Soured cream, to serve

1 Melt the butter with the oil then add the onions and cook until soft – about 5 minutes.
2 Add the potatoes and stock and cook for about 20 minutes until the potatoes are soft.
3 Add the lovage and cook for another 5 minutes.
4 Blend well, reheat, check the seasoning and serve with the soured cream swirled in.

Chives and Garlic chives

Add these herbs to any salad or other cold dish for flavour – they will enlighten any egg mayonnaise or vegetable dip. They are also an invaluable garnish for any soup, risotto or pasta dish.

Parsley

The ubiquitous herb. A traditional béchamel based parsley sauce is hard to beat when mad with the fresh herb. The tightly curled varieties have the stronger flavour.

Chive oil

30 g chives
½ tsp sea salt
200 ml olive or rapeseed oil

1 Blend the chives and salt together in a blender until well mixed.
2 Leaving the motor running, gently drizzle in the oil to create a smooth mixture.
3 Strain through a fine sieve into a jug, then transfer to a bottle or squeezy dispenser.
4 Use immediately or keep in the fridge for up to a week, but remember to bring to room temperature before using.

In the Kitchen

More ways with parsley apart from the standard béchamel based sauce:
· Add to a gnocchi mixture.
· Add to fried rice or tabbouleh with some pine nuts.
· Use in place of basil in a pesto.
· Add to a salsa verde with other fresh herbs.
· Add to any egg dish hot or cold.
· Make a flavoured oil, as for chives.

Basil

Pick basil leaves as you need them. If you take the tips from plants it will encourage side shoots to grow. Basil is the herb that arguably best accompanies warm weather crops such as tomatoes, peppers and courgettes. A salad of tomatoes, avocado and mozzarella is incomplete without basil. Make your own pesto as for rocket (p 187). Like parsley it works well in gnocchi. Basil is also a good partner for strawberries. Marinade them with sugar, the chopped herb and some lime juice.

Chervil

Use chervil in any dish that partners well with celery.

Coriander

The ideal herb for Asian dishes of all kind, whatever their level of heat. Even better when made into a chutney.

CORIANDER CHUTNEY

Mix 50 g of chopped coriander leaves and stems with 1 tsp of chopped fresh ginger, ½ a fresh green chilli and a crushed garlic clove. Add 1 tsp lime juice, 2 or 3 tbsp of water and ½ tsp ground cumin. Season well with salt and blend or grind in a pestle and mortar until smooth.

Dill

Always good with any cucurbit (especially gherkins in a pickle) and all kinds of fish, including smoked salmon, trout and mackerel and seafood. It is an essential ingredient of tartar sauce. Add to mayonnaise for a tasty potato salad or butter to finish a pasta dish. Chop and mix with soured cream or Greek yoghurt and season well for a dip or sauce. Dill will also add flavour to an avocado dip.

Fennel

Choose the greenest and freshest fennel leaves for the kitchen and use them in all the same ways as dill. Harvest the seeds (they will self-seed abundantly if allowed to fall into the soil) and shake them out onto newspaper and leave them to dry fully. Use them in stir fries and Asian dishes of all kinds.

Borage

The leaves of borage are always best when young – older ones can be tough and hairy. An essential addition to Pimm's, borage is also an unusual but delicious addition to soups and stews and can be added to cream cheese and yoghurt. Try it chopped over shellfish dishes.

Horseradish

You will need a strong fork or spade to dig up horseradish. In late autumn a good ploy is to lift and store roots in boxes of peat through the winter. From these will come the roots to start off next year's crop. In the kitchen it needs to be peeled and grated. It is best used fresh, but can be preserved in white vinegar.

FLOWERS

The seeds of some flowers can be harvested and eaten.

Nasturtium seeds

Ripe seeds allowed to dry out thoroughly for a couple of days can be sprinkled with salt then pickled in flavoured vinegar – they taste like capers. Or use them at once for homemade capers.

Sunflowers

Once seeds have formed on a variety you are certain is edible, be sure to harvest them before they become bird feed. An easy way of harvesting them is to enclose the heads in a piece of muslin, or pick them when the seeds are formed but not yet ripe and dry them indoors. Lightly salted they are a perfect snack or addition to a salad.

Capers

50 ml white pickling vinegar

50 ml water

½ tsp caster sugar

½ tsp sea salt

150 g nasturtium seeds, washed

1 tsp chopped dill, chervil or fennel leaf

1 Boil the vinegar, water, sugar and salt, then add the seeds and herbs. Spoon into a sterilized, lidded jar, and leave for 2 weeks in the fridge.

FRUIT

Fruit needs to be harvested carefully to prevent it from damage and any bruised fruit used or preserved as soon as possible. Jam is the obvious way of using fruit, but many fruits freeze well. Strawberries are the least successful as they contain the most water and stone fruits will need to be pitted. Use labelled bags or put fruit on trays to open freeze them first. Another alternative is to preserve fruit in alcohol. If you use a spirit of at least 35 per cent ABV, such as brandy or gin, there is no need to add extra sugar, and it will keep for years, but sour fruit such as gooseberries may benefit from extra sweetening. Fruit makes excellent sauces and can be the basis of savoury preserves such as chutneys.

KNOW YOUR FRUIT

For jam the amount of pectin in the fruit is key to its setting quality. For some (especially strawberry) you may need to add extra pectin. Apples are high pectin so can be a useful addition. Pectin is usually highest in slightly underripe fruit.
- High pectin: Currants of all colours, gooseberries, apples, pears, plums, damsons and gages.
- Medium pectin: Raspberries, loganberries, tayberries and boysenberries.
- Low pectin: Strawberries, blueberries blackberries and cherries.

SOFT FRUIT

Soft fruit of all kinds makes great jam and ice cream and is the basis for sauces and delicious desserts such as mousses and fools.

Strawberries

If you can't get to your allotment every day, it is worth picking strawberries just as they are beginning to ripen and finishing them off indoors even if you don't get 100 per cent good fruit. Frozen, defrosted strawberries are almost always mushy but puréed make a superb sauce (cold or hot) to accompany everything from ice cream to chocolate dishes of any kind.

Strawberries make a great addition to a basic sponge:

Strawberry cake

115 g unsalted butter, softened

200 g caster sugar

2 large eggs, separated

Zest of 1 large lemon

1 tsp vanilla extract

½ tsp cinnamon

200 g self-raising flour

1 tsp baking powder

125 g soured cream

250 g strawberries, halved

1 Heat the oven to 180°C and line a 20 cm cake tin with baking parchment.
2 Beat the butter and sugar until light and fluffy, then add the egg yolks, lemon zest and vanilla.
3 Fold in the flour in 2 batches, then add egg whites and soured cream. Beat on low speed until smooth but be careful not to overbeat.
4 Add half the batter to the pan, followed by half the strawberries. Add the rest of the batter to the pan then, put the remaining strawberry halves on top. Sprinkle with sugar.
5 Bake for 35-45 mins until a skewer comes out clean. Cool in the tin before turning out.

"Soft fruit of all kinds makes great jam and ice cream...."

Raspberries, Loganberries and Hybrid fruit

A raspberry crop will need picking every few days. If rain has made the fruit soggy it can be picked and puréed or discarded, depending on its condition. Raspberries keep their texture much better than strawberries when frozen and defrosted. Loganberries, boysenberries and tayberries have an even firmer texture than raspberries, and all of them freeze better. A summer pudding made with frozen allotment raspberries and redcurrants makes a Christmas or New Year treat.

Gooseberries

Although you need the nimbleness of bare hands for fruit picking, protect your arms with long sleeves when harvesting gooseberries. Topped and tailed they freeze very well – a perfect crumble or fool ingredient. To take the edge off their tartness, you can mix them with apples. Because they are so tart gooseberries make a great sauce if cooked and puréed to serve with fatty proteins such as goose, pork and mackerel. For a fool, use the rhubarb recipe (p 198), but omit the ginger and add 2 or 3 tablespoons of elderflower cordial. Serve with shortbread fingers. Jams and chutneys are other popular uses.

Raspberry jam

500 g fresh ripe raspberries
500 g granulated white sugar

1 Put the fruit and sugar into a heavy based pan and heat very gently until the sugar has dissolved and the fruit is soft.
2 Bring to the boil and boil rapidly for 5 to 7 minutes, skimming off any scum that comes to the surface.
3 Test for setting by spooning a teaspoon of jam onto a saucer cooled in the refrigerator. Leave it to cool a little, then push it with your finger. The surface of set jam will wrinkle.
4 Pour into warm, sterilized jars, seal and label."

"Protect your arms with long sleeves when harvesting gooseberries...."

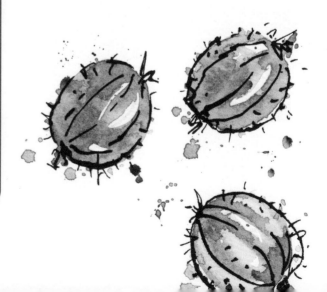

Blackcurrants

Many of the newer blackcurrant varieties bear fruit that ripens simultaneously on each bunch or strig, which makes harvesting much easier. Use a fork to remove fruit from each strig. When using blackcurrants for jam cook them gently before you add the sugar to prevent them becoming hard. Add a blackcurrant purée to a cheesecake or use them to flavour a spirit such as vodka.

Red and White currants

When really ripe and ready, redcurrants are a deep crimson. While they are usually harvested like blackcurrants there is no need to strig them if you're going to make redcurrant jelly. Ripe white currants are in fact a pale cream colour.

Redcurrant jelly

1 kg redcurrants, rinsed
Granulated white sugar

1 Put the fruit and 500 ml of water into a heavy based pan. Allow to boil then reduce the heat and simmer gently for 30-40 minutes until pulpy. Stir frequently and be careful not to burn.
2 Spoon the mixture into a jelly bag and allow to drip overnight – at least 12 hours.
3 Pour the liquid into a measuring jug then pour into the cleaned pan with 400g of sugar for every 500 ml of juice.
4 Cook, stirring, over a low heat to dissolve the sugar, then bring to the boil and cook until setting point is reached. (See raspberry jam p 196).
5 Pour into sterilized jars, seal and label.

Blackberries

Unless you have thornless ones, pick blackcurrants with care. They freeze well, keeping their texture and flavour. With apples they make one of the best jellies and a crumble without compare.

Blueberries

Make sure you pick your blueberries before the birds get them. They are also good for freezing and jam. Use them in muffins and cheesecakes as well as fresh and whole.

Cape gooseberries

Left in their husks, cape gooseberries will keep for several weeks. If not eaten raw they are best used for jam.

Rhubarb

From spring onwards, pull and trim rhubarb as you need it (the poisonous leaves can safely go into the compost heap or bin) but by July or August it will almost certainly be stringy and past its best. Rhubarb freezes well either chopped and raw or cooked and makes good jam and chutney. It is surprisingly good added to a lamb casserole. For a crumble try mixing it with chopped stem ginger, or add cinnamon and flaked almonds to the topping.

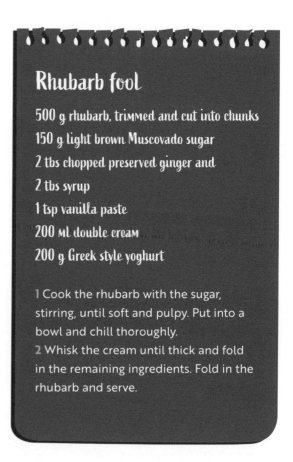

Rhubarb fool

500 g rhubarb, trimmed and cut into chunks
150 g light brown Muscovado sugar
2 tbs chopped preserved ginger and
2 tbs syrup
1 tsp vanilla paste
200 ml double cream
200 g Greek style yoghurt

1 Cook the rhubarb with the sugar, stirring, until soft and pulpy. Put into a bowl and chill thoroughly.
2 Whisk the cream until thick and fold in the remaining ingredients. Fold in the rhubarb and serve.

TREE FRUIT

On the allotment, the biggest problem with harvesting tree fruit can be getting to the crop before it falls to the ground. Windfalls can be used as long as they have not decayed or been eaten by birds or insects. Throw the worst into the compost.

Apples

Windfalls are inevitable and if not too decayed can be used at once. For good keeping, however, you need perfect, unbruised fruit picked by hand. A perfectly ripe apple will come away easily when you put a hand under it and twist a little. To make harvesting from high branches easier it helps to have some kind of apple picker. A popular design consists of a bag attached to circle of prongs at the end of a long handle. As the prongs are pressed against the fruit stems the fruit falls into the bag. Before storing, make sure apples are clean and dry then place them stalks downwards in cardboard trays so that they do not touch, or wrap them individually in newspaper. Keep an eye on them over the winter and get rid of any rotting ones before decay spreads to their neighbours.

In the Kitchen

A few of the many good uses for apples:
• Make a chutney, adding plums and onions.
• Dip apple slices or rings in a mixture of lemon juice and water and dry them overnight in a very low oven. Store in airtight jars.
• Add to blackberries for a pie or crumble.
• Make them into juice.
• Make a Dorset apple cake, an apple charlotte or a tarte tatin.
• Use them for apple fritters.
• Instead of pastry, top an apple pie with meringue.

Plums

Plums freeze well (ideally halved and stoned), either raw or cooked but they do need to be picked before they fall off the trees and before the wasps can get to them. All are good for jam and chutney, pies and crumbles.

Cherries

Fresh, ripe cherries are a real treat if you are able to harvest them successfully. On the allotment you may well need a ladder unless your trees are smaller varieties. They freeze well and it is worth the time consuming effort of stoning

In the Kitchen

WAYS WITH PLUMS

· Cook them with a little sugar, some red wine vinegar and a couple of cloves as an accompaniment for roast or grilled pork or roast lamb.
· Make a plum ketchup.
· Use plums as an alternative to strawberries (see p 195) in a fruited sponge cake.
· Make a plum tarte tatin.
· Chop and mix them with strawberries to top a pavlova.

Cherry clafoutis

450 g ripe cherries, stoned

3 eggs

100 g plain flour

3 tbs caster sugar, plus extra for sprinkling

½ tsp vanilla paste

450 ml full fat milk

15 ml kirsch or brandy (optional)

Unsalted butter for greasing

1 Heat the oven to 190°C
2 Beat together the eggs, flour, milk and vanilla to make a smooth batter, then stir in the spirit, if using.
3 Generously grease a 1 L baking dish with the butter. Put in the cherries, followed by the batter.
4 Bake in the oven until the batter is brown on top and set through.
5 Sprinkle with sugar and serve warm.

For extra flavour, soak the cherries in the kirsch or brandy for 1-2 hours before using them.
This also works very well with other allotment fruits such as plums or blueberries.

them beforehand. If you make jam from cherries you will need to add pectin. The classic dessert made with cherries is the clafoutis.

Pears

Pears need to be picked during autumn before they are ripe and stored in a cool, dark place until ready to eat. Tall trees inevitably present the same challenges as apples but can be harvested with an apple picker. Once the flesh near the stalk begins to soften they can be brought into a warm room to finish ripening for a couple of days but will then need to be eaten, cooked, preserved or frozen quickly.

In the Kitchen

• Oven dry pear slices as for apples.
• Pickle pears in vinegar with cloves, allspice and root ginger.
• Add to apples for a jam or to tomatoes for a chutney.
• Poach pears in red or white wine or a sherry.
• Serve in a salad with blue or goat's cheese with walnuts and land cress.

"Pears need to be picked in the autumn before they are ripe...."

Index

OTHER RUTH BINNEY TITLES FROM RYDON PUBLISHING:

WEEDS ON TRIAL
Ruth Binney
ISBN 978-1-9108-21275

FLOWER GARDEN SECRETS
Ruth Binney
ISBN 978-1-910821-42-8

GARDEN WILDLIFE ON TRIAL
Ruth Binney
ISBN 978-1-910821-29-9

**AMAZING AND
EXTRAORDINARY FACTS:
THE ENGLISH COUNTRYSIDE**
Ruth Binney
ISBN 978-1-910821-45-9

**AMAZING AND
EXTRAORDINARY FACTS:
THE SCOTTISH COUNTRYSIDE**
Ruth Binney
ISBN 978-1-910821-43-5

**AMAZING AND
EXTRAORDINARY FACTS:
COASTS**
Ruth Binney
ISBN 978-1-910821-39-8

PLANT LORE AND LEGEND
Ruth Binney
ISBN 978-1-910821-10-7

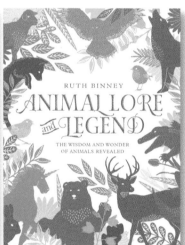

ANIMAL LORE AND LEGEND
Ruth Binney
ISBN 978-1-910821-15-2

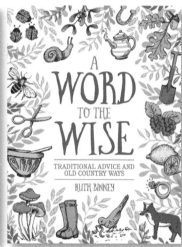

A WORD TO THE WISE
Ruth Binney
ISBN 978-1-910821-11-4

RYDON
PUBLISHING

For more great books visit our website at www.rydonpublishing.co.uk

About the Author

Ruth Binney has been studying plants and enjoying gardening since childhood and has cultivated two allotments in London and one in Dorset. Since graduating from Cambridge in Natural Sciences she has enjoyed a successful career in publishing, as an editor of illustrated non-fiction and an author. Her most recent titles include *Weeds on Trial, Garden Wildlife on Trial, Plant Lore and Legend* and *Flower Garden Secrets.* She now lives near her family in Cardiff.